brilliant

PRINCE2™

PRINCE2™

What you really need to know about PRINCE2

Stephen Barker

Harlow, England • London • New York • Boston • San Francisco • Toronto • Sydney • Auckland • Singapore • Hong Kong
Tokyo • Seoul • Taipei • New Delhi • Cape Town • São Paulo • Mexico City • Madrid • Amsterdam • Munich • Paris • Milan

PEARSON EDUCATION LIMITED
Edinburgh Gate
Harlow CM20 2JE
United Kingdom
Tel: +44 (0)1279 623623
Web: www.pearson.com/uk

First published 2013 (print and electronic)

© Pearson Education Limited 2013 (print and electronic)

The right of Stephen Barker to be identified as author of this work has been asserted by him in accordance with the Copyright, Designs and Patents Act 1988.

Pearson Education is not responsible for the content of third-party internet sites.

ISBN: 978-0-273-75053-6 (print)
      978-0-273-75056-7 (PDF)
      978-0-273-75055-0 (ePub)

British Library Cataloguing-in-Publication Data
A catalogue record for the print edition is available from the British Library

Library of Congress Cataloging-in-Publication Data
Barker, Stephen, 1964-
  Brilliant Prince2 : what you really need to know about Prince2 / Stephen Barker.
    pages cm
  ISBN 978-0-273-75053-6 (pbk.) -- ISBN 978-0-273-75056-7 (PDF) -- ISBN 978-0-273-75055-0 (ePub)
  1. Project management. I. Title.
  HD69.P75B378 2013
  658.4'04--dc23
                            2012051016

10 9 8 7 6 5 4 3 2 1
17 16 15 14 13

Print edition typeset in 10/14pt Plantin Std Regular by 30
Print edition printed and bound in Great Britain by Henry Ling Ltd, at the Dorset Press, Dorchester, Dorset

NOTE THAT ANY PAGE CROSS-REFERENCES REFER TO THE PRINT EDITION

For Ellie and Will

Contents

About the author

Stephen Barker is a project management professional with over 20 years of experience. His clients range from small technology start-ups to large government departments. He has a wealth of practical experience of applying PRINCE2 to real-world projects.

You can contact the author on brilliantp2@gmail.com

Acknowledgements

This book wouldn't have been written without an invitation from Pearson to take on this challenging project. So thanks are due to Sam Jackson, who made the approach and then nurtured the idea through its initial stages. Since then, a host of her colleagues have had a hand in navigating the manuscript through the publication process. This process hasn't always been straightforward, and considerable persistence and patience have been required by all concerned.

The offer to write *Brilliant PRINCE2* came from the success of *Brilliant Project Management*. So this book owes much to the experience of co-writing its predecessor. Project management is an exciting and colourful profession, and *Brilliant Project Management* took the view that there's no reason why a book on the subject should be dull and theoretical. The sales figures back-up this argument, and *Brilliant PRINCE2* tackles its subject in a similar spirit.

This book also owes a lot to the many people I've worked with on projects over the last twenty years or so. This practical experience has been invaluable and has given me plenty of food for thought. I'm a firm believer in the adage that you learn most when things go wrong – and at least there's a good war story to be had on the *odd* occasion that things haven't quite worked out as planned.

Final thanks go to Wendy, for encouraging me to take the time out to write, and for being a firm but fair reviewer. I'm also grateful for the loan of her copy of the official PRINCE2 manual, whenever I've mislaid mine. It hasn't been returned in quite the same condition as it was when I first borrowed it.

CHAPTER 1

Introducing
PRINCE2™

Welcome to the family

It is common sense to take a method and try it. If it fails, admit it frankly and try another. But above all, try something.

Franklin D. Roosevelt (1882–1945)

Introduction

If you've picked up this book, it's a fair bet that you've heard of PRINCE2™. Maybe you've recently attended a training course or bought the official manual, and are pondering 'what next?' Perhaps you're just wondering what all the fuss is about.

You certainly find yourself in good company. The PRINCE2 authors say that it's used in more than 20,000 organisations across 150 countries. Many regard it as the world's leading project management method. Certainly, its popularity demands a closer look by anyone involved in commissioning or running projects.

Any constructive advice is undoubtedly worth considering. Experience shows that an on-target delivery can't be taken for granted. In fact, some surveys put the project failure rate as high as 70%. In particular, organisations spending public money seem prone to spectacular disasters. Relative perceptions might be corrected though if the private sector had to open its doors too!

PRINCE2 – the name originates from **PR**ojects **IN** a **C**ontrolled **E**nvironment – is a UK government response to the challenge of successful project delivery. It's built on the belief that a systematic approach is vital, and that this must incorporate real-world lessons on what brings the right results.

The top five reasons for using a project management method:

1 The team can get on with delivery, rather than debating the approach from first principles.

2 The participants understand their roles, and they don't have to learn them each time they pick up a new project.

3 Best practice can be captured and encouraged.

4 There's a reliable basis for reporting progress and an 'apples with apples' comparison can be made across a portfolio.

5 Re-usable techniques, tools, and templates are given a natural home.

What's a project?

Projects are used to bring about a change that's intended to benefit the sponsoring organisation. Here's the definition provided by the PRINCE2 manual:

A *project* is a temporary organisation that is created for the purpose of delivering one or more business *products* according to an agreed *Business Case*.

(As a bonus, the above introduces the name that PRINCE2 uses for a deliverable: a *product*.)

In contrast with business-as-usual activities, a **temporary** nature is an important feature. A project is set up with a specific purpose in mind and then disbanded once its objective has been met. PRINCE2 emphasises the importance of a clearly defined beginning and end. This ensures the right preparations are made at the outset, and there's a clean hand-over at the conclusion.

What makes a project a project helps to explain why events don't always run smoothly. A couple of other defining characteristics bring their own risks:

● **Uniqueness**. Whilst projects have similarities, no two are the same. So there's always an element of journeying into the unknown. Therefore, the outcome can't be predicted with 100% certainty.

- **Cross-functional teams**. To achieve the right blend of skills and knowledge, resources are drawn from across the organisation – and perhaps from outside of it too. Securing the right people can be problematic, and there's an art to moulding an effective team from individuals working with each other for the first time.

However, these problems aren't insurmountable. Many projects are a success, and their winning formula can be bottled up, shared and repeated.

What does PRINCE2 bring to the party?

PRINCE2 equips its clientele with a structured approach to setting up and running projects. Its method is built upon project management best practice. The following are included as part of the package:

- a standard lifecycle to take a project from start to finish;
- a set of processes that narrate the activities undertaken at each stage;
- descriptions of the *products* that are needed if work is to be properly planned and managed;
- an organisational structure, with a definition of the roles and responsibilities involved.

There are also practical techniques for developing business cases, planning and controlling work, and monitoring progress. The components that make up the PRINCE2 framework are described in detail in the next chapter.

Projects vary enormously in the core content of their work. For example, the specialist tasks and outputs for a marketing campaign have little in common with the technicalities of an IT development, or the nuts and bolts of a house build. However, PRINCE2 restricts its focus to management controls. Since these are universally applicable, the method can be adopted for any kind of project. So whilst PRINCE2 originated in the public sector, it has been taken up by all kinds of organisations and has a large following in the commercial world.

What's in this book?

This book is a practical guide to PRINCE2. It describes all of the important aspects of the method; including the processes, *products* and people involved. There's plenty of handy advice too on how to apply the theory in the real world.

The book's structure follows the PRINCE2 lifecycle, so the journey can be traced from beginning to end. Nonetheless, chapters are clearly aligned with PRINCE2 topics, so these can also be dipped into as required. The PRINCE2 subjects covered in each chapter are advertised as it begins.

brilliant tip

On first introduction, the PRINCE2 jigsaw might appear complex. However, all of its pieces fit together beautifully. The 'PRINCE2 on a page' figure on page 202 is the picture you'd hope to find on the puzzle's box. You might like to fold down the corner of that page, for easy reference.

Finally, a word on PRINCE2 terminology. Some of its terms are in common use, but have a precise meaning in the PRINCE2 context, such as *Project Manager* and *product*. Others are unique, like *Project Board* and *Managing a Stage Boundary*. In the interests of clarity, all the jargon is highlighted using *this font*.

This book is for you if you're:

- Looking for a quick and accessible introduction to PRINCE2.
- Wanting to put the theory into practice.
- Studying for a PRINCE2 qualification and in search of a friendly companion to the official text.
- Looking for a guide that's a little less formal – and more lightweight – than the manual.

To get to grips with PRINCE2, the best place to start is with an appreciation of its various components and how they work together. This is the subject of the next chapter.

CHAPTER 2

The PRINCE2 framework

The big picture

PRINCE2 topics covered in this chapter:

- *Principles*
- Project lifecycle
- *Themes* and *Processes* (overview)

Those are my principles, and if you don't like them . . . well, I have others.

Groucho Marx (1890–1977)

Introduction

PRINCE2's advice on how a project should be managed is built around three fundamental building blocks:

- **Principles** – universal guidance that show the way for all projects.
- **Themes** – tailored project management techniques that need to be applied consistently throughout.
- **Processes** – activities to take a project from start to finish.

These fit neatly together. The guiding *principles* drive the design of *processes* and the *theme's* techniques. The latter are also tailored for a snug fit with the way in which projects are organised and run. Lastly, *processes* make extensive use of PRINCE2's toolkit as a venture is guided from its early preparation, through initiation and delivery, and on to closure. Figure 2.1 illustrates the relationship.

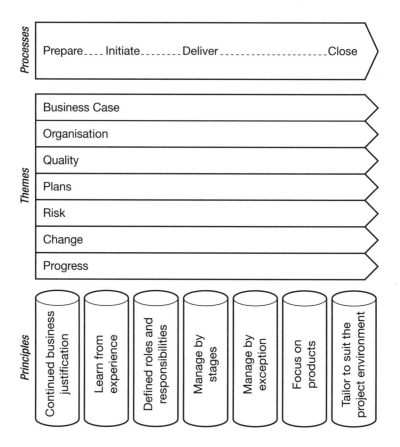

Figure 2.1 The fundamental PRINCE2 building blocks

This chapter explains PRINCE2's guiding *principles*. It also describes the project lifecycle, and provides an overview of *themes* and *processes*.

PRINCE2 principles

Over the years, considerable experience has been accumulated on what contributes to project success and the pitfalls to avoid. The PRINCE2 community has drawn on this knowledge to arrive at important lessons for everyone. Some have been captured in the form of general principles of good management practice. PRINCE2 picks out seven to underpin its whole approach. They are:

- *Continued business justification*
- *Learn from experience*
- *Defined roles and responsibilities*
- *Manage by stages*
- *Manage by exception*
- *Focus on products*
- *Tailor to suit the project environment*

Within any PRINCE2 project these principles are taken seriously. As the manual says, 'If a project does not adhere to these principles, it is not being managed using PRINCE2, because the principles are the basis of what defines a PRINCE2 project.' However, this is more than simply a get-a-tick-in-the-box exercise. They're valuable pointers to what makes for a successful outcome and, therefore, deserve a regular re-visit.

brilliant tip

In need of a quick project health check? Use the seven PRINCE2 *principles* as a handy checklist to assess what shape your project is in. Give yourself a pat on the back where you find you're following the golden rules, and stick at it. Where you fall short, consider how best to close the gap.

So exactly what elements of best practice are highlighted, and how does this advice get applied? PRINCE2 kicks off with the most basic question: 'Is there any point?'

Continued business justification

PRINCE2 principle

A PRINCE2 project has continued business justification.

Source: © Crown Copyright 2009. Cabinet Office.

Any project should have a sound rationale for its existence. Broadly speaking, this means that its expected benefits outweigh its estimated cost – and there's a reasonable prospect of a successful outcome. Its business justification also needs to explain why, of the alternatives available, the recommended option is the best one.

Since projects rarely take place in isolation, this assessment includes considering what contribution will be made to the organisation's overall strategy. This additionally provides an opportunity to identify dependencies or overlaps with other initiatives.

PRINCE2 supplies an approach for developing a *Business Case*, with plenty of advice on what the analysis should address and how the results could be presented. It also explains how to link benefit forecasts with measures of actual results.

Clearly a project should only be taken forward where there is a credible trade-off between benefit, cost and risk. However, this isn't a one-off exercise. As work progresses, much more becomes known about the time and resources needed to deliver. Perhaps the forecast benefits will be called into question too. The outside world doesn't stand still either. For example, the rosy business case for printing thousands of 'Paris 2012' t-shirts ahead of time lost *some* of its gloss once the winning Olympic bid was announced, and champagne corks started popping in London.

In some organisations, once a project has started it's almost impossible to get it stopped – even when it's plain to see that the original business justification has been fatally undermined. Often the team gets so wrapped up in wrestling a growing set of problems that it loses sight of the bigger picture. It can also be tough for individuals who've made a strong personal commitment to then to have a hand in cancellation.

So for PRINCE2, business justification isn't just thought about at the beginning. It's formally revisited at multiple pre-defined points – hence, *continued business justification*. There's no issue with the justification evolving during the course of a project; but the benefit, cost and risk equation must always stack up.

Learn from experience

PRINCE2 principle

PRINCE2 project teams learn from experience: lessons are sought, recorded and acted upon throughout the life of the project.

Source: © Crown Copyright 2009. Cabinet Office.

All projects are unique and, therefore, involve entering uncharted territory. The collective knowledge of those involved offers valuable insight into what works well and what's just waiting to go wrong. So this experience is a major factor in project success.

When it comes to benefiting from experience, PRINCE2 provides the team with a significant head start. Its management framework embeds what's been learned on countless projects. However, this generic guidance needs to be supplemented with local knowledge. The nature of the work, the sponsoring organisation, and the individuals involved are all relevant when identifying which specific lessons to draw upon.

Tapping into all of the experience available – and particularly that of those not directly involved in the project – requires the team to be proactive. It also pays to remember that it's not all doom and gloom. Learning from experience isn't just about identifying past mistakes. It's equally important to recognise what's gone well, so that past successes can be repeated.

Extracting maximum benefit from this exercise also requires getting beyond the superficial symptoms of triumphs and disasters. The most useful lessons will be found through uncovering the underlying root causes for what went well and not so well.

brilliant tip

Harvesting lessons doesn't have to be an onerous, bureaucratic exercise. Indeed, a few informal one-to-one discussions with a few key players can yield more useful information than a large set-piece meeting.

Capturing lessons learned starts at the outset of a PRINCE2 project, with them then being sought all the way through to closure. This enables experience to be captured whilst it's fresh in everyone's mind, and also provides an immediate opportunity to apply what's been learned.

Defined roles and responsibilities

PRINCE2 principle

A PRINCE2 project has defined and agreed roles and responsibilities within an organisation structure that engages the business, user and supplier stakeholder interests.

Source: © Crown Copyright 2009. Cabinet Office.

For a project to be delivered successfully, those involved need to understand the specific roles they'll play. A management structure also needs to be established to oversee the work. Achieving this degree of choreography can present a real challenge. Resources are typically drawn together from different parts of an organisation (perhaps even from different organisations); each person bringing with them a variety of expectations and working styles. It's also usual to employ a mix of full-time and part-time resources. Most wouldn't choose this as their ideal starting point for building a slick and cohesive project team.

PRINCE2's response to this challenge is to provide a standard set of roles, and an explanation as to how these should be organised. Its starting point is to divide the project world up into the following three primary stakeholders:

- *Business sponsors* who set objectives and ensure the investment represents value for money.
- *Users* who exploit the project's outputs to gain the intended benefits.
- *Suppliers* who provide the resources and expertise to build what's needed (these may be internal or external).

These stakeholders have representation within the *project management team* to ensure the interests of those commissioning, supplying and using the project outputs are balanced.

The organisational structure mandated by PRINCE2 ensures that it's clear who's responsible for managing what. It also supports effective decision making; striking the right balance between freedom to get on with the job and intervention when it's needed.

Manage by stages

PRINCE2 principle

A PRINCE2 project is planned, monitored and controlled on a stage-by-stage basis.

Source: © Crown Copyright 2009. Cabinet Office.

Breaking a sizeable task down into manageable chunks is a well recognised technique for dealing with something that seems daunting. For projects, this approach brings some particular advantages. First, it enables planning to be carried out at an appropriate level of detail; with the current phase of work having a detailed plan, and later steps being described at summary level. This is a sensible approach because effort spent specifying distant work in detail is almost certain to be wasted.

Whilst you can reasonably plan exactly what you want to do next Tuesday, you're unlikely to commit to an hour-by-hour schedule for this time next year.

Second, breaking up a project provides a series of natural checkpoints between each step. These encourage the management team to consider the bigger picture at regular points. In particular, they reinforce the message about ensuring *continued business justification.*

PRINCE2 implements this *principle* by requiring a project to be broken down into *management stages.* The right level of planning is achieved through a combination of a high level *Project Plan,* together with a detailed *Stage Plan* for the current work phase.

Stages also provide the basis for formal management controls. These are embedded within PRINCE2's processes for running stages and for regulating the transition from one to the next.

Manage by exception

PRINCE2 principle

A PRINCE2 project has defined tolerances for each project objective to establish limits of delegated authority.

Source: © Crown Copyright 2009. Cabinet Office.

In the interests of efficient and effective delivery, the right balance has to be struck between giving individuals enough freedom to be productive, whilst maintaining sufficient controls to ensure the project doesn't go off the rails. Taking a management perspective; you'd also want your (hopefully) highly capable senior managers to get involved when their expertise or guidance is absolutely required, but not to get tied up in unnecessary detail.

PRINCE2 achieves this balance using the approach of *delegating authority* through the agreement of *tolerances.* Put simply, individuals are able to exercise their own judgement provided the work they're responsible for remains within agreed boundaries.

Tolerances are described in terms of the extent of deviation that's permissible before upward escalation is required. They're defined for the following six plan objectives:

Objective	Tolerance	Example
Time	Time before and after a target completion date	Between –5 and +2 working days of 6th June
Cost	Cost below and over a planned budget	Between –20% and +10% of a €100,000 budget
Quality	Deviation from a quality target	Testing reveals no major defects and less than 5 minor defects
Scope	Deviation from an agreed product	Merchandise design meets all mandatory requirements and at least 75% of desirable requirements
Risk	Extent of risk exposure	No significant health and safety risks to personnel identified
Benefit	Deviation from planned benefits	Forecast sales increase to remain at least 80% of that planned

To avoid shutting stable doors long after horses have bolted, the controls implemented track *forecast* performance against agreed tolerances – not just the current position. This provides the opportunity to intervene early, and to oversee corrective action before a problem worsens.

The management team also requires on-going assurance that the mechanisms used to control delegated authority are robust. After all, there's nothing worse than being constantly re-assured that everything is on track, only to find out you're accountable for a disaster that's been brewing undetected.

Focus on products

PRINCE2 principle

A PRINCE2 project focuses on the definition and delivery of products, in particular their quality requirements.

Source: © Crown Copyright 2009. Cabinet Office.

What would be your top project management tip? How about: a project should be driven by what it needs to *produce*, and not a preoccupation with what it needs to *do*? This advice gets to the very heart of project management. It ensures that the required end result is agreed and planned for before everyone rushes off to start work. As the management guru Stephen R. Covey urges, 'begin with the end in mind'.

One of PRINCE2's primary strengths is that it's built around this philosophy. In fact, the manual says that 'The "product focus" supports almost every aspect of PRINCE2: planning, responsibilities, status reporting, quality, change control, scope, configuration management, product acceptance and risk management.' That's quite a list!

In a PRINCE2 project, deliverables are described using *Product Descriptions*. The scope of what's included in a *Product Description* can be customised to suit, but as a minimum you'd expect to find the following:

Element	Description
Identifier	A code that uniquely identifies the *product*
Title	The name of the *product*
Purpose	A summary of why the *product* will be constructed
Composition	A list of the components that make up the *product* (in the case of a document its table of contents could be used)
Derivation	The information or material source(s) that will be used during the construction of the *product*
Format and presentation	A description of the physical attributes of the *product* (for example 'a presentation style report')
Quality criteria	The measures that will be used to ensure that the *product* is fit for purpose (for example, 'Can the document be readily understood by someone with no technical knowledge?')
Quality method	The manner in which the *product* will be assessed against its *quality criteria* (for example 'Conduct formal quality review meeting with senior management team')

A set of *Product Descriptions* is a great tool for ensuring that the expectations of those on the supplier side and those on the receiving end are aligned from the outset. In particular, time invested in jointly crafting *quality criteria* will give a handsome return. This provides a forum for flushing out misunderstandings and ambiguities, which would otherwise come back to haunt the project after the damage has already been done. It also establishes the baseline for which the project will ultimately be judged: a fit-for-purpose delivery.

Tailor to suit the project environment

PRINCE2 principle

PRINCE2 is tailored to suit the project's environment, size, complexity, importance, capability and risk.

Source: © Crown Copyright 2009. Cabinet Office.

One of PRINCE2's assets is that it's a generic project management method, and so can be applied to all sorts of ventures. However, this flexibility does carry a small price tag. Thought needs to be given to the situation specifics, and how these should shape tactics for extracting maximum value from the method.

The *project management team* needs to agree how the use of PRINCE2 will be configured to suit its particular needs. This will be influenced by factors such as the size and scale of the project, the level of risk being taken on, and the collective experience available.

PRINCE2 is very clear that tailoring doesn't translate into simply cutting out parts of the method that don't appeal. Instead roles, *processes* and *products* are implemented in a pragmatic way. This might include:

- Combining roles; for example, the *Project Manager* takes on the *Project Support* role too.
- Running a project with a single delivery stage.
- Combining *products* used to manage the project, for example, consolidating all of the control logs in one place.
- Reducing the formality of some *products*; for example, providing reports verbally or via email (whilst ensuring that a record of key actions and decisions is still maintained).
- Using terminology more familiar to the audience in support of, or as a substitution for, PRINCE2 specific terms.

PRINCE2 themes

Building on its *principles*, PRINCE2 provides a set of project management techniques to apply throughout the life of a project. It calls these '*themes*', and there are seven of them. Whilst many of the core ideas contained within the *themes* could be applied to any project, PRINCE2 describes them in a way that's designed to dovetail with its delivery *processes*. For example, putting mechanisms in place to ensure a fit-for-purpose delivery is a must-have for any project, but the *Quality* theme techniques are described from the perspective of PRINCE2's *product* focus.

Here's a list of the *themes* with a brief description of each one:

- **Business Case** (Why?). Supporting the *principle* of *continued business justification*; the techniques used to demonstrate whether or not the project is worth investing in, and to ensure that this question is kept under review.

- **Organisation** (Who?). Supporting the *principle* of *defined roles and responsibilities*; the project roles that are required, and how these are used to provide a clear division of accountabilities and responsibilities.

- **Quality** (What?). Starting with the *principle* of *focus on products*, the techniques that are used to ensure that the project's outputs are fit for purpose.

- **Plans** (How? How much? When?). A set of techniques for planning how a project is going to deliver its *products*, what resources this will require, and how long it will take.

- **Risk** (What if?). A set of techniques for anticipating events with the potential to throw a project off course, and for making intelligent decisions about how to deal with these.

- **Change** (What's the impact?). A set of techniques for assessing potential changes to the project, and to ensure that these are dealt with appropriately.

- **Progress** (Where are we now? Where are we going? Should we carry on?). Supporting the *principles* of *continued business justification* and *manage by exception*; a set of techniques for capturing actual and forecast performance against the plan, and to deal with any significant deviations.

To provide some useful context, this book slots discussion of PRINCE2's *themes* at appropriate points in the journey through the project lifecycle. Here's where the detail is provided:

Chapter	PRINCE2 themes
Chapter 3	*Organisation*
Chapter 5	*Business Case*
Chapter 7	*Plans, Quality* and *Risk*
Chapter 9	*Change* and *Progress.*

PRINCE2 processes – the big picture

So, to recap, PRINCE2 has some common sense underlying *principles*, and a set of handy project management techniques. But how does PRINCE2 actually drive a project from A to B? The answer is: through a set of defined *processes*. These spell out what needs to be done, who should do it, and the end result being strived for.

Before getting into the detail, it's worth stepping back to take in the big picture. Any project management framework that's going to earn its keep needs to provide a sensible path – or *lifecycle* – for getting from start to finish. A reputable lifecycle recognises that there's a logical and efficient sequence in which work should be undertaken, and that there are some tasks that absolutely must be done before others. Furthermore, built-in quality checks should tell you if you're *really* ready to move on.

PRINCE2 lays out the project lifecycle as:

- **Pre-project**. Gaining formal control and establishing there's an outline case for venturing further.
- **Initiation Stage**. Developing delivery plans and a detailed *Business Case*, and deciding if the investment needed is justified.
- **Delivery Stage(s)**. Executing the project using one or more *management stages*, and then closing it.

Each phase of the lifecycle is completed using a number of pre-defined *processes*. These incorporate the formal controls required to govern progress from one step to the next.

Figure 2.2 The PRINCE2 project lifecycle

Pre-project

Pre-project is PRINCE2's starting place for running with an idea, and it provides the point at which formal control is first established. It's recognised that just because someone has asked for a project to be kicked off, it doesn't necessarily mean that it's the best use of time and resources. A fundamental objective of this first stage is to confirm that there's a viable outline *Business Case* and, therefore, that the next stage is warranted.

At the outset a business sponsor – or *Executive* in PRINCE2 terms – is appointed. They're given accountability for the project's success, and have the final say in any important decisions. An early task is to set up the *Project Board,* which will provide overall direction, with the *Executive* acting in the role of chair.

Soon after, a *Project Manager* is recruited to oversee work on a day-to-day basis. Top of the to-do list is preparation of an outline plan for the project. This is required to support the outline *Business Case,* and provides an initial view on timescales, cost estimates and key risks. The process of sketching out a delivery plan may also help to refine the benefits that might be expected. For example, these could be dependent upon the solution envisaged or the likely timelines involved.

As well as developing an outline plan for the project, the *Project Manager* has to produce a detailed plan for the next stage. This documents how a final decision on whether or not to proceed will be reached. It also lays the necessary groundwork to ensure progress can be made without delay if the green light is given.

Initiation stage

If it's agreed that the outline *Business Case* shows promise, it's time to move on to the *Initiation Stage*. The next key objectives are to determine if the initial justification withstands closer scrutiny, and to develop a decent delivery plan. This stage lays the foundations needed for a successful project. If it isn't undertaken diligently the risk of failure is greatly increased.

The *Initiation Stage* is also the right point at which to start giving some careful thought about who's got an interest in the project, and how these people will be brought on board. It's an area that needs investment upfront to ensure customers' needs are met. It's even not too early to start thinking about the consultation required to ensure a smooth transition to operational use.

Even with a sound *Business Case* and a robust delivery plan, there's still an important question outstanding before the go-ahead can be given: can the project be afforded? The source of funding needs to be identified and agreed. Where significant reliance is placed on use of existing resources, this would include securing them. This might extend beyond personnel to include equipment and facilities.

Finally, the *Project Board* will want to ensure the right controls are in place to protect the investment it's considering making. These would include mechanisms for managing risks and issues, and for assuring quality.

If the detailed *Business Case* wins the argument for the project, it's given clearance for take-off.

Subsequent delivery stages

The *delivery stages* that follow are where the 'real work' gets done. Depending on the nature of the challenge, it may have been agreed to split this effort into multiple *stages*.

The *Project Manager* is responsible for assigning work to the team, and tracking and reporting progress against the plan. Interventions are made when issues are run into or risks demand a response. Records are maintained to support project controls and to provide an audit trail that demonstrates they're effective.

As each stage approaches its conclusion, the *Project Manager* prepares a detailed plan for the next. Before allowing work to move on, the *Project Board* satisfies itself that:

- the current stage has successfully delivered all of the *products* it set out to;
- there's a credible plan for the next stage; and
- there's still benefit in running the project.

Final delivery stage

The concluding phase of a project can be a tricky one as the team members' attention starts wandering in the direction of the next exciting opportunity. However, there's important work to be done – and much more than organising the end of project party! In the *Final Delivery Stage*, the project needs to complete hand-over of its *products*, ensuring that the outputs are truly owned. This includes being confident that the results of all that hard work will continue to operate once the project team has been disbanded – and for the foreseeable future.

It's likely that payback from the project will only finally be attained some time after closure. However, as part of the wrap up benefits already delivered are documented, and the future forecast position is given a last sanity check. Importantly, accountability is established for continuing to measure benefits post shut down. Records are also tidied up and archived.

The project is only allowed to disband once the *Project Board* has confirmed that it has delivered what it committed to, and that all of the formal closure tasks have been ticked off.

PRINCE2 processes – the smaller picture

So what are the PRINCE2 processes, and how do they fit within the lifecycle described above? Having seen that there are seven principles and seven themes, it comes as no surprise that PRINCE2 arms you with seven processes. Here they are:

- **Starting up a Project**. Determining if a project looks viable and worthwhile.

- **Directing a Project**. Making key decisions and exercising overall control.

- **Initiating a Project**. Establishing what needs to delivered, what this will take, and whether or not there's sufficient business justification to proceed further.

- **Controlling a Stage**. Managing the project day-to-day against the plan.

- **Managing Product Delivery**. Setting the team to work and verifying the results.

- **Managing a Stage Boundary**. Reviewing a concluding stage and preparing for the next.

- **Closing a Project**. Making a final hand-over and ensuring the project is ready to close.

Some processes are specific to a stage, and others are run more than once. The grid in Figure 2.3 below shows which processes get used where.

You're not left to work out for yourself what each *process* involves. PRINCE2 specifies the activities required, and recommends actions for each one. As you'd expect from the *focus on products*, it's made clear what each activity needs as an input, and which *products* get created or updated as a result.

This book steps through PRINCE2's lifecycle, and describes each *process* as it first comes into play. Here's where you'll find the detail:

Chapter	PRINCE2 themes
Chapter 4	*(Pre-project): Starting up a Project.*
Chapter 6	*(Initiation Stage): Managing a Stage Boundary.*
Chapter 8	*(Subsequent Delivery Stage(s)): Controlling a Stage; Managing Product Delivery.*
Chapter 10	*(Final Delivery Stage): Closing a Project.*

Directing a Project runs across the lifecycle. So its part in the story is picked up at each step.

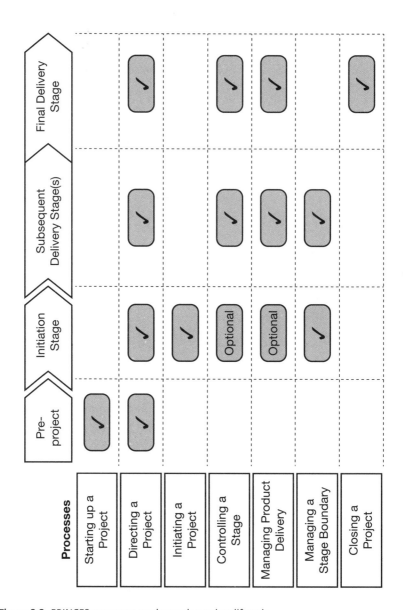

Figure 2.3 PRINCE2 processes used over the project lifecycle

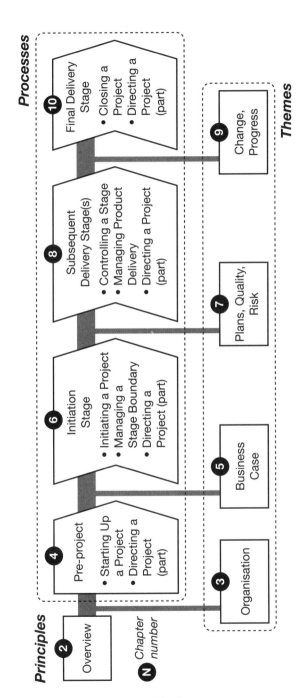

Figure 2.4 How PRINCE2 topics are organised by chapter

Summary

PRINCE2 is a flexible, generic method for managing projects. So it's relevant whether you're putting up a building, implementing an innovative IT system, or opening a new shop.

It's based upon a set of fundamental *principles*, which set the ground rules for how a project should be set up and run. *Themes* provide project management tools and techniques. They're tailored to suit the *processes* that are used to plan, evaluate, control and deliver.

There's a logical sequence to take a project from its early stages through to formal closure. Emphasis is placed on up-front preparation and always ensuring there's sufficient business justification for the next investment step. The correct balance is struck between giving individuals the freedom to deliver, and having the right controls in place to intervene when necessary.

A defining feature of PRINCE2 is its *product* focus. The philosophy that a project should be driven by what it needs to *produce* shapes nearly every aspect of the approach.

However, a project is nothing without its people; who need to be organised and clear on their roles and responsibilities. This important topic is the subject of the next chapter.

 **brilliant** recap

PRINCE2 has seven **principles**, seven **themes** and seven **processes**:

Principles	Themes	Processes
● Continued business justification	● Business Case	● Starting up a Project
● Learn from experience	● Organisation	● Directing a Project
● Defined roles and responsibilities	● Quality	● Initiating a Project
● Manage by stages	● Plans	● Controlling a Stage
● Manage by exception	● Risk	● Managing Product Delivery
● Focus on products	● Change	● Managing a Stage Boundary
● Tailor to suit the project environment	● Progress	● Closing a Project

CHAPTER 3

PRINCE2 and people

Meet the team

PRINCE2 topic covered in this chapter:

- *Organisation* theme

Life's like a play; it's not the length but the excellence of the acting that matters.

Seneca (ca. 4 BC–AD 65)

Introduction

Before delving into PRINCE2's processes, its runners and riders deserve an introduction. An understanding of how a PRINCE2 team is organised provides important context for how projects are delivered. As advertised by the *defined roles and responsibilities* principle, there's a critical success factor to digest too. For a team to act like a team, and not a bunch of individuals, everyone has to know what's expected of them. This has to be established from day one and maintained through to closure.

PRINCE2 theme

The purpose of the *Organisation* theme is to define and establish the project's structure of accountability and responsibilities (the who?).

Source: © Crown Copyright 2009. Cabinet Office.

Within its *Organisation* theme, PRINCE2 sets out an organisational structure for managing projects. Some roles support the different levels of management, from those in possession of the big picture through to

Team Managers overseeing individual tasks. There are also positions to provide quality assurance, to assist in governing project change, and to give administrative support.

In order to cater for varying degress of size and complexity, flexibility is provided through the definition of *roles* rather than individual *jobs*. Most can be shared or combined to suit the circumstances. The exceptions are the *Executive* and *Project Manager* positions, which each require a single name in the frame and with no sharing allowed. This avoids short circuiting controls or – perhaps even worse – sinking to management by committee. A single *Project Manager* also ensures that it's crystal clear who gives the lead to the delivery team.

Customers, suppliers and hangers-on

The PRINCE2 project organisation is built on a customer/supplier model. It assumes that there's a client who'll say what's wanted from the project, and justify the resources needed; and that someone suitably qualified will step forward to deliver against the requirement. Throughout PRINCE2, this customer/supplier relationship is represented by three categories of stakeholder:

- **Business** – those given customer responsibility for ensuring that the investment is justified and the approach represents value for money.
- **User** – those within the customer organisation who will use the project's outputs; or end up with responsibility for operating, maintaining and supporting the result.
- **Supplier** – those from the supplier organisation bringing the delivery skills and resources.

The interests of these three groups must be satisfied for a project to be considered a success. However, they're not alone: others will be impacted by the project or have a wider interest in it. So to ensure that everyone's needs are understood, and to smooth the path ahead, PRINCE2 supplies tactics to engage with the full range of supporters and detractors.

Project management team

To achieve the right stakeholder representation, PRINCE2 sets its management organisation up as a team effort. This also addresses a practical consideration: even if it were desirable, most business leaders don't have the bandwidth to take personal charge of the day-to-day running. The team structure goes hand-in-glove with delegation and control processes.

The *project management team* consists of:

- *Project Board* (with *Executive, Senior User* and *Senior Supplier* representatives)
- *Project Manager*
- *Team Managers* (optionally)
- *Project Assurance*
- *Change Authority*
- *Project Support*

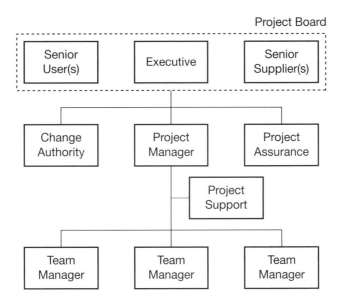

Figure 3.1 Organisational structure of the project management team

Source: Based on material from the PRINCE2 manual. © Crown Copyright 2009. Cabinet Office.

If at all possible, continuity should be maintained once individuals are slotted into roles. However, this stability can't be guaranteed. Some churn of management resources might even be appropriate as the project evolves. Disruption is minimised if changes can be synchronised with stages. Even in circumstances when a swap of personnel is outside of the project's control, clearly described roles and well documented plans smooth the transition.

The management line

A *Project Board* is established early on to take overall responsibility for the project. It has authority to make decisions within the high level boundaries agreed with the organisation; for example regarding the budget available and the scope that must be tackled. The *Board* comprises three roles: *Executive*, *Senior User* and *Senior Supplier*.

The members of the *Project Board* are collectively responsible for the success or failure of the project. Speaking with one voice, they provide direction and delegate management responsibilities appropriately. The *Board* secures the necessary funding and resources, and ensures that stakeholders are effectively managed at all times.

'Project board qualifications'

A *Project Board* capable of fulfilling its role will be able to answer the following questions with a resounding *yes*:

- Are its members sufficiently well placed in the organisation to have the **authority** to make decisions and to commit resources?
- Do they have the **availability** to take on their roles and to be successful in them?
- Can its members **delegate** effectively; striking the right balance between intervention and freedom to operate?
- Does the *Board* have the **credibility** needed for its decisions to be respected by the team and the wider organisation?

The **Executive** represents the top-down interests of the organisation. The role has particular responsibility for scrutinising *continued business justification*. This starts with ensuring the project stays focused on its forecast benefits and the objectives set in support of these – and that they continue to be aligned with the organisation's strategy. It also includes pushing for value for money.

Ultimate accountability for the project ends up at the **Executive's** door. This person is therefore a key decision maker with the casting vote. As the PRINCE2 manual nicely puts it, 'the Project Board is not a democracy'. This role gets filled at day one, and the **Executive** then gets a significant say in who else joins the *project management team*.

It shouldn't happen on a programme (but did) . . .

An ambitious business change programme was drawing to a close. A final lessons learned exercise was run to pick over the bones of the dozen or so projects involved. Some had done a cracking job, others had stumbled over the finishing line, and there had been one spectacular disaster. The big question was: what combination of factors led to success or failure? An assurance team poured over the data; considering size, complexity, duration, *Project Manager* experience and much more.

A remarkable fact emerged. To predict with 100% certainty how a project was going to perform, you would only have needed to know one thing at its outset: the credentials of the person assigned to the role of *Executive*.

The role of *Executive* is a critical appointment. Finding someone competent who's well placed within the organisation and has a strong personal motivation to succeed gives the best possible start.

The **Senior User** role represents those who will use and look after what's delivered. **Product** specifications are overseen, and quality checks monitored, to secure a fit-for-purpose result. This includes facilitating the commitment of user resources. The **Senior User** also has responsibility for specifying benefits and then demonstrating that these have been realised (a duty which may well run beyond project closure). To achieve the appropriate coverage where a wide variety of user interests exist, the role may be shared across more than one individual.

The **Senior Supplier** role represents those engaged in the construction effort, from design through to hand-over for operational use. It's common to add specialist maintenance and support personnel to this remit too. This is where responsibility rests for designing feasible solutions and providing realistic delivery estimates. The **Senior Supplier** is then on the hook for providing promised resources, and ensuring that **products** get built and hit their quality targets. The role could be taken on by more than one person; for example, to cover the respective interests of those with build and support duties.

 **tip**

Keeping it in the family?

When an external supplier is being used, a decision has to be made whether or not to invite an outsider onto the **Project Board** to take up a **Senior Supplier** role. On the plus side, this promotes co-operation and seamless decision making. A potential drawback is that a third party could gain access to sensitive information. There's no right or wrong answer, and the judgement on which way to go rests with the **Executive**.

A **Project Manager** is appointed to take care of day-to-day running of the project on behalf of the **Project Board**. Management responsibilities are delegated within agreed boundaries, and the **Project Manager** is given the helm for the execution of most PRINCE2 **processes**. The **Project Board** operates on an exception basis, only directly intervening when the project is in danger of heading outside of pre-set tolerances.

The **Project Manager** may in turn delegate responsibility for managing a specific package of work to a **Team Manager**. The latter is charged with successful creation of one or more **products**. This role can be used to facilitate distribution of effort, and to bring expert skills and know-how to the project. It may also address geographical constraints, such as where a team is spread across sites or even countries. Where **Team Managers** aren't assigned, the **Project Manager** supervises the team directly.

 **tip**

Some people are creative types, some love detail, and others like nothing better than plugging away at a problem until it's cracked. Teams tend to work best when there's a good mix of characters involved. When building a team look to get the right blend.

Supporting roles

The *Project Board* carries with it a *Project Assurance* role. Each *Board* member is ultimately responsible for the quality of the project outputs from their respective business, user or supplier angle. To gain access to specialist expertise, or to reduce the burden of work, additional resources may be recruited to perform assurance tasks. Each appointed helper reports to the *Project Board* member representing the relevant area of interest.

However it's resourced, the independence of the assurance function must be maintained. In particular, work can't be delegated to the *Project Manager*. This avoids giving someone the job of marking their own homework.

 **tip**

Encourage a collaborative environment where it's the norm for the *Project Manager* and others to seek out timely advice from *Project Assurance*. This is much more productive than living with a combative assurance function that seems to delight in only finding fault once the damage has been done.

During project initiation the *Project Board* may also decide to delegate some of its change control responsibilities through establishment of a *Change Authority*. This body takes on some of the work to assess potential project changes and to make decisions about appropriate responses. As with *Project Assurance*, this move creates additional bandwidth and allows additional expertise to be brought to the party. It's a role that the *Project Manager* might assist with.

The last of the roles that PRINCE2 specifies within the *project management team* is that of **Project Support**. Responsibility for this rests with the *Project Manager*, and encompasses just about anything needed to keep the organisation firing on all cylinders. This might range from providing administrative support (e.g. maintaining quality records) to offering project management advice (e.g. on planning techniques). If the *Project Manager* isn't successful in securing some help with this role, they end up being a one-stop shop for all things project-management related.

The view from 30,000 feet to three

A project needs to be effectively managed at a number of levels concurrently; from maintaining alignment with strategic goals through to controlling the delivery of individual *products*. PRINCE2's organisational structure is designed with this need in mind; and implemented through the roles defined for the *Project Board, Project Manager* and *Team Manager*.

There are four levels of management. The first is supplied by the wider organisation. Sitting outside of the project, **corporate or programme management** is responsible for commissioning the venture and setting the boundaries within which the *Project Board* operates. Levels two to four are provided by the *project management team*.

- **Directing**. The *Project Board* sets the overall direction and is accountable for project success
- **Managing**. The *Project Manager* oversees the project on a day-to-day basis and is responsible for ensuring that the agreed *products* are produced in line with the performance targets set
- **Delivering**. Under the supervision of a *Team Manager* (or the *Project Manager*), team members are responsible for constructing individual fit-for-purpose *products* within time and cost targets

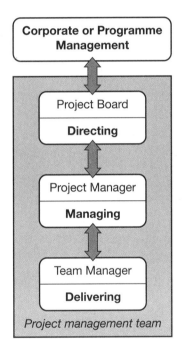

Figure 3.2 PRINCE2 management levels

Friend or foe?

Those directly involved in, or impacted by, a project extend beyond the *project management team* and the heady heights of sponsoring senior managers. Some will be obvious; for example the project doers and all of the users. Others may take a little investigation to flush out; especially if they sit outside of the organisation.

A well organised project understands who its stakeholders are and the nature of their interest. This analysis is used to prepare strategies for engaging and communicating with them. The necessary tasks are then incorporated within the project's plans.

The first step is to prepare an inventory of those people (or groups of people) that might have an interest in the project and/or have the potential to influence its outcome. Each stakeholder's interest is then described, along with other information that can be used to shape engagement plans and to set priorities. This might include record-ing whether they're considered to have a positive or negative attitude towards the project, and the degree of influence that they're able to wield. Here perceptions are taken into account, since these will motivate stakeholders – not objective facts and figures alone.

Next, strategies for influencing and interacting with stakeholders are developed. For example, ways of harnessing the enthusiasm of on-side opinion leaders might be found, and schemes to win over semi-hostile critics hatched. However, there's more than Machiavellian plotting to be done. The nuts and bolts of how direct contributors are going to get involved deserves at least as much attention.

Working with stakeholders requires two-way communications. In-coming and out-going information needs are analysed, so that these can be fed into the project's overall *Communication Management Strategy*.

Engagement and communication activities are included in plans as they're developed, using the respective strategies as a guide. During a project, relationships with stakeholders are kept under review so that the approach can be refined where needed.

 **example**

Stakeholder analysis

There is a variety of techniques for analysing stakeholders. The example below plots where they sit in terms of their attitude towards a project and their ability to influence the outcome. The resulting picture assists in planning stakeholder engagement. It illustrates individual stances and offers a visual representation of the overall position too.

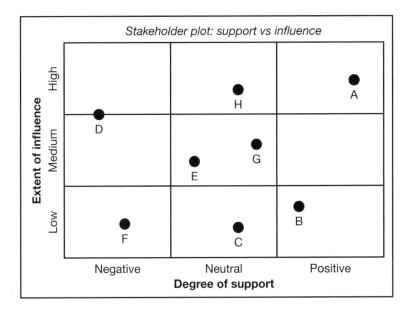

Stakeholder plot: support vs influence

So, for example, it looks as though influential Stakeholder D presents the greatest threat. Their less than enthusiastic view needs to be turned around – or failing that maybe there's a way to reduce their clout. There are also a lot of 'undecideds' (C, E, G, H). Perhaps a simple communications exercise could sweep this bunch up and turn them into supporters.

Summary

PRINCE2 establishes a clear management structure for projects. It identifies the roles that are required and specifies their individual responsibilities. So everyone involved knows what's expected of them and how they're expected to work with others. Both small and large projects are organised along the same lines, with staffing flexibility achieved through positions that can be shared or combined.

An unambiguous line of accountability runs from the *Project Board* to the *Project Manager*, and down to *Team Managers*. This is the path along which delegation flows and exceptions are raised. Whilst management by committee is avoided, overseeing a project is a team effort. Supporting roles bring additional skills and remove bottlenecks.

A PRINCE2 project is organised around the needs of its stakeholders. It's set up so that both customers and suppliers have a voice. Others with an interest or influence aren't forgotten. Steps for identifying and analysing *all* stakeholders are provided, and these culminate in plans for handling interactions and communications.

 brilliant recap

- The *Project Board* directs the show. The *Senior User* and *Senior Supplier* have their say, but the *Executive* is the ultimate arbiter.

- The *project management team* roles comprise: *Project Board, Project Manager, Team Manager, Project Assurance, Change Authority* and *Project Support.*

- The roles of *Executive* and *Project Manager* must each be filled by a single (different) person.

- Stakeholder analysis extends beyond the world of the *project management team* to embrace the needs of *everyone* with interest or influence.

CHAPTER 4

Pre-project

Sorting the wheat from
the chaff

PRINCE2 topics covered in this chapter:

- *Starting up a Project* process
- *Directing a Project* process (*Overview* and *Authorise initiation* activity)

Price is what you pay. Value is what you get.

Warren Buffett (1930–)

Introduction

In an ideal world, projects would emerge in an orderly fashion. Most would be born out of a well thought out strategy, and designed as co-ordinated steps towards the greater good. Only occasionally would projects be required to deal with an emergency, or to seize an opportunity that had suddenly appeared.

As we know, reality is somewhat different. Projects spring into life in all kinds of interesting and challenging ways. Many initiatives have been brewing for some time, and perhaps have had several false starts. Some get underway based on little more than a rough idea that someone senior has cooked up. Others are simply a knee-jerk response to a crisis. Even when an organisation has got around formally to commissioning a project, you can't be sure that it's necessarily a great idea.

Whilst the definition of a project includes the idea of a 'defined beginning', in practice, this usually has to be manufactured. This marks the point at which a line is drawn under previous dubious history, and the initiative is brought under proper control.

PRINCE2 calls this point in the evolution of a venture *Pre-project*. The fundamental objective here is to filter out projects that can't demonstrate sufficient promise. This phase is executed via a couple of processes:

- *Starting up a Project*
- *Directing a Project*

The bulk of the work is achieved through the *Starting up a Project* process. This includes the analysis steps to support the decision whether or not to proceed to formal initiation. The *Directing a Project* process is kicked off too, and is then used throughout the project lifecycle. With the clue being in the name, one particular activity is of particular relevance at this point: *authorise initiation.*

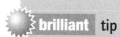 **tip**

Create an environment where a decision to reject a project is seen as a positive outcome and not as a failure. It's just as important to stop resources being wasted on ventures that will never make the grade, as it is to steer worthwhile endeavours through the process.

Starting up a project

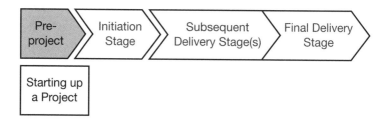

Source: © Crown Copyright 2009. All rights reserved. Material is reproduced with the permission of the Cabinet Office under delegated authority from the Controller of HMSO.

The *Starting up a Project* process provides the mechanism for ensuring that only worthwhile projects are taken to the next stage. It also lays the necessary groundwork to establish what this would entail. The trick here is to do enough to determine whether or not a project has legs, whilst avoiding burning resources on investigating proposals that have no future.

Objectives for starting up a project

- Ensuring that an outline justification for the project exists (or agreeing that the proposal should be shelved).
- Assessing options for delivering the project and making a recommendation.
- Documenting a project outline to set the scope.
- Preparing a detailed plan for the next stage, and securing the individuals who are required to undertake and to manage the work.
- Obtaining the sign-offs required to allow the project to be initiated.

The process is triggered when someone with the authority to commission a project issues terms of reference. These include a sketch of the idea and its objectives, and some broad pointers to what should happen next. PRINCE2 calls this document a *project mandate*. There's no set format. However, sufficient information is required to enable investigation to start, and this includes supplying the name of the person who's expected to fill the *Executive* role. The *mandate* may originate from within the organisation's management set-up. Alternatively, if the project is just one component of a wider venture the starting gun will be fired by that programme's management team.

Once the *Executive* and *Project Manager* are in place, work can start on developing the project approach and outline *Business Case*. The rest of the *project management team* is recruited too, and a plan for the *Initiation Stage* is needed.

PRINCE2 defines the *Starting Up a Project* process using six activities:

- *Appoint the Executive and the Project Manager.*
- *Capture previous lessons.*
- *Design and appoint the project management team.*
- *Prepare the outline Business Case.*
- *Select the project approach and assemble the Project Brief.*
- *Plan the Initiation Stage.*

The key output is a *Project Brief,* which holds the results of the analysis. Sometimes a project is run as part of a wider programme of work that's already established. In this case the *Brief* is supplied directly by the commissioning programme. The process then turns into a validation exercise to determine if what's been handed down requires any refinement.

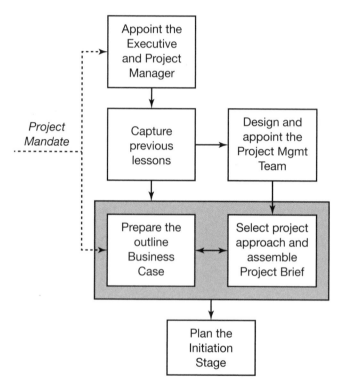

Figure 4.1 PRINCE2's recommended path through Starting up a Project activities
Source: Based on material from the PRINCE2 manual. © Crown Copyright 2009. Cabinet Office.

Appoint the executive and the project manager

The buck needs to stop somewhere, and as we've seen in Chapter 3, that's at the *Executive's* desk. So filling this role is a logical first step. In fact, a prerequisite for the project having a sound business justification is that a suitably qualified person is willing to take on this accountability. The *Executive* is appointed by whoever commissioned the project.

Once the *Executive* is in place, their immediate priority will be to find someone to delegate day-to-day management to. Enter the *Project Manager.*

PRINCE2 recommends that the *Executive* makes the appointment. Whilst many organisations have their own systems for assigning *Project Managers*, it's reasonable for the *Executive* at least to vet the proposed candidate. After all, the *Executive* and *Project Manager* will need to form an effective working relationship, and to maintain this through thick and thin.

 **tip**

As *Executive*, you suspect a questionable assignment has been made when the *Project Manager* . . .

- seems more surprised than you that they've been asked to manage the project;
- has already found a way of alienating your PA before even getting started;
- is proud of the fact that their diary is frequently double and triple-booked;
- arrives at your first meeting with no visible means of recording anything agreed or actioned;
- sees communication by anything other than email as a measure of last resort;
- believes 'organised chaos' is a serious management technique (with the 'organised' part being optional).

At this point, PRINCE2 recommends that a *Daily Log* is set up. This is a central repository that can be used for holding information on actions and events. It can also be used to hold risks and issues until formal registers have been established.

Capture previous lessons

In line with the *Learn from Experience* principle, this early stage is the right time to begin the search for relevant, reusable lessons. An effort should be made to track down others within the organisation with useful know-how. Perhaps they've been involved in a similar project, are subject matter experts in a relevant field, or have simply watched many projects come and go. There might also be some valuable insights to be gained from suppliers or other organisations that have faced similar challenges (even competitors). So it's time to dust off those personal networks and then to see what can be learned.

brilliant tip

Building up a wide range of connections early on pays dividends in all sorts of ways. It's an excellent opportunity to raise the profile of your project, and so reduce the risk of others straying onto your patch. Your contacts will be prompted to ask 'Have you spoken to . . .?' when they spot overlaps. Best of all, it's surprising how many people you come across early on, who then turn out to be handy resources at a later date.

PRINCE2 recommends that lessons are recorded in a *Lessons Log*. This will then be grown throughout the project for the benefit of the team, and for others that take an interest.

Design and appoint the project management team

Having got the *Executive* and *Project Manager* in place, it's time to decide upon the best management structure. As described in Chapter 3, PRINCE2 provides a framework designed to balance the needs of the sponsoring organisation, the people that will use the end results, and those making the delivery. This is used to build a team that's capable of effective and timely decision making, and whose members are clear on their respective roles and responsibilities. It also sets up reporting and communications lines.

Some aspects of the PRINCE2 organisation aren't negotiable, for example, having a *Project Board* and a single *Project Manager*. In other areas, there are specific options to consider, including:

- Do any of the *Project Board* members want to delegate their assurance activities to some additional resources?
- Will the *Project Manager* be supported by *Team Managers* when it comes to delivering the project outputs?
- Is the *Project Manager* likely to be successful in off-loading some *Project Support* tasks?

Where the answer to these questions is *yes*, the corresponding roles are defined and willing volunteers sought.

As far as possible, specific individuals should be identified for each of the *project management team* roles. Confirmation is required that they're both willing and able to participate. However, it's not always possible to get names in the frames for every role. For example, where a *Team Manager* is to be provided by an as yet to be selected supplier, the person to fill the role will have to go by the initials 'TBD'.

Prepare the outline business case

A project that makes it through to the *Initiation Stage* is given the chance to develop its comprehensive *Business Case*. However, just an outline is needed for the decision to move forward or to be abandoned. (The whole story on *Business Cases* can be found in the next chapter.)

It's the *Executive's* responsibility to prepare the answer to the crucial 'why?' question. This task starts with the project's *mandate* and consideration of the reasons for its commissioning. Based on the information that can be obtained from a light touch analysis, and data supplied by the *Project Manager*, an initial view is taken on the balance between cost, benefit and risk. Approval for the outline *Business Case* is sought from the relevant corporate or programme management.

Alongside the outline *Business Case,* and taking direction from the *Senior User* and *Executive,* the *Project Manager* produces the *Project Product Description.* This provides the highest level view of what the project will deliver. It includes:

- a description of the major *products;*
- the customer's view on the quality targets that need to be hit;
- the criteria the customer will use to accept or reject the results;
- how the process of customer acceptance will be managed.

Select the project approach and assemble the project brief

Having got a picture of what has to be delivered, some thought can be given to how this is going to be achieved. Options for tackling delivery work are always available. These include the techniques and tools to be used, and how resources and materials will be sourced. There are also some more fundamental considerations, such as whether to build from the ground up, or to adapt an existing asset.

Some choices will already be pre-determined. For example, many organisations have a strategy of buying in packaged software rather than coding it themselves. In this environment, a proposal to deliver a system by recruiting an army of developers is unlikely to get far. Other considerations include requirements to comply with standards set within the organisation, and those enforced through legal requirements and regulatory frameworks.

Practical constraints also help to limit the range of feasible options to review. For example, the implications of the funds and skills available could heavily influence the choice of approach. A re-visit of lessons learned is always a good idea too. Experience may show that some routes give a better chance of success than others.

Decisions on the approach, and the results of the other start-up activities, are recorded in a *Project Brief.* This document collates the information needed for the initiate or abandon decision.

 **example**

Project brief – table of contents

A *Project Brief* gathers together the analysis work for a decision on whether or not to proceed to initiation. It's assembled by the *Project Manager* during *Pre-project* and would typically include the following sections:

Section	Typical contents
Background	The background to the project and a summary of progress made to date
Project Objectives and Desired Outcomes	A description of what the project is setting out to achieve; covering time, cost, quality, scope, risk and benefit objectives
Outline Business Case	A high level summary of the business justification for the project (based on current information), and the rationale for selecting the recommended delivery option
Project Scope	A clear description of the boundary that will be drawn around the scope of the project, identifying the key items that are both inside and outside its remit
Project Product Description	Identification of the major *products* the project will produce, with the criteria the customer will judge whether or not a fit-for-purpose delivery has been made
Project Tolerances	The important boundaries set for the project; described in terms of time, cost, quality, scope, risk and benefits
Project Approach	A description of the approach that will be taken to meeting the project requirements
Project Organisation	A diagram showing how the *project management team* is organised, together with a description of all of the important roles
Risks, Constraints and Assumptions	A list of the key risks and constraints identified to date, with a description of any important assumptions that have been made at this stage
Stakeholders	A list of the people and groups that have an interest in the project, with a brief description of the nature of their interest

Plan the initiation stage

The *manage by stages* principle calls for PRINCE2 projects to be planned on a stage-by-stage basis. Accordingly, the final activity of the *Starting up a Project* process is to *Plan the Initiation Stage*. This step ensures that it's known in advance what initiation entails and how long this phase of work is expected to last. Preparation in advance also allows the lead time between approval being given and the initiation process getting underway to be minimised.

It shouldn't happen on a project (but did) . . .

A *Project Manager* joined a project on what she thought was day one. However, she was surprised to find that a team of analysts had already been recruited and was busy analysing. On investigation, it emerged that those responsible for the project portfolio had anticipated approval, and thought it would be great to get the resources on board *slightly* ahead of time. Unfortunately, they hadn't considered what would happen if the commissioning body sat on its hands for a couple of months. This made for a lively first *Project Board* meeting when the *Project Manager* had to explain why 25% of the budget had already been spent.

Preparation for the next stage is essential. But committing time and resources without authorisation is a dangerous game.

The required level of management control is decided. If the *Initiation Stage* is seen as a significant undertaking in its own right (e.g. because of the complexity or degree of risk), then the stage plan might incorporate the two PRINCE2 processes that are used to supervise delivery work: *Controlling a Stage* and *Managing Product Delivery*.

Planning out the *Initiation Stage* is tackled in the same way that PRINCE2 approaches any planning work. How to go about this is covered in Chapter 7. In summary, though, this entails:

- identifying and analysing the *products* needed;
- designing activities and understanding their dependencies;
- estimating resource requirements and the timescales involved;
- building a work schedule;
- documenting the plan, and getting it reviewed and approved.

The *Initiation Stage Plan* is submitted, along with the *Project Brief*, to the *Project Board* for the go/no-go decision.

Directing a project – opening act

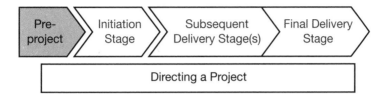

Once the *Starting up a Project* process is complete, a decision is required as to whether or not to proceed any further. This is the first of a number of important management decisions that take place at major project milestones.

In PRINCE2, the process that implements this oversight is *Directing a Project*. It swings into action at the conclusion of the *Starting up a Project* process, and then runs through to closure.

Objectives for *Directing a Project*:

- Providing the authority for the project to move from one stage to the next, from initiation through to closure.
- Making sure that the right management direction and controls are applied.
- Monitoring the on-going viability of the *Business Case*.
- Providing central co-ordination with the wider organisation.
- Overseeing planning for how actual versus anticipated benefit delivery will be assessed post-project.

The controls offered by the process are aligned with the *Project Board's* responsibilities, and are consistent with the *manage by exception* principle. *Directing a Project* lays out the points in the lifecycle at which the *Board* has specific, high level decisions to make. Escalation paths are also defined to deal with exceptions and the interventions that may then be required. Lastly, whilst the *Project Board* has its important official role to play, there's also room for friendly informal advice. The process includes the routes by which the *Project Manager* can take advantage of the knowledge and expertise of *Board* members.

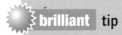

brilliant tip

Timely advice and guidance, and informal contact between *Project Board* and *Project Manager*, are great ways to harness collective expertise. All concerned just need to ensure that this informal channel isn't used so extensively that it undermines proper controls.

A particular responsibility of the *Project Board* is to keep the *Business Case* under review, and this is prompted throughout the process. Accepting that the *Board* will have a personal commitment to the project, it's still well placed to call time if it sees that the original business justification has evaporated. It brings the expertise of the *Executive* and *Senior User*, and also has the advantage of being one step removed from the daily cut and thrust.

Remembering that projects don't take place in isolation, the *Project Board* also provides the formal channel of communication with corporate or programme management. These interactions also appear within the process.

The *Directing a Project* process is built around five activities:

- *Authorise initiation* – used during *Pre-project*.
- *Authorise the project* – used during *Initiation Stage*.
- *Authorise a Stage or Exception Plan* – used from *Initiation Stage* onwards.
- *Give ad hoc direction* – used throughout the project.
- *Authorise project closure* – used during the *Final Delivery Stage*.

Its key outputs are approvals and management decisions – plus some friendly advice and guidance.

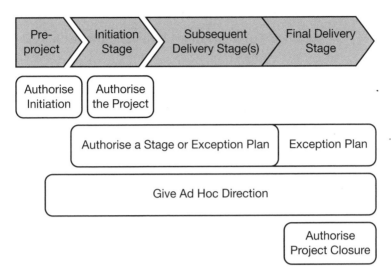

Figure 4.2 Directing a Project activities across the PRINCE2 lifecycle

Source: © Crown Copyright 2009. All rights reserved. Material is reproduced with the permission of the Cabinet Office under delegated authority from the Controller of HMSO.

Authorise initiation

The first critical decision point has now been reached, and the *Project Board* is accountable for granting (or withholding) the approval required to move on to project initiation.

Arriving at the right decision involves a review of the *Project Brief* and *Initiation Stage Plan* that have been prepared. The *Project Board* may choose to enlist some expert assistance before making a call. For example, if the pitch under consideration is dependent upon some complex technology, a suitably qualified technical expert may be engaged to confirm the feasibility of what's being proposed.

 **action:** Good questions to ask before authorising initiation

- Do the promised benefits sound plausible? Is there some logic behind the upside – or have numbers been plucked out of thin air?

- Does the proposed solution to the requirements look feasible? Is there a better way of achieving the same end result – or at least getting close?

- Are any of the assumptions made suspect? If those assumptions turn out to be wrong, is the proposal holed below the water line?

- Does the plan for the next stage include everything that's needed to arrive at a detailed *Business Case* and a credible delivery plan? Do the time and resources allocated for this look realistic?

- Is there evidence of early commitment from the key players? If not, does this raise cause for concern?

If the *Project Board* gives the go-ahead, it signs off the *Project Brief* and *Initiation Stage Plan.* This includes acceptance of the proposed scope and approach, and the controls for the next stage. The appointments to the *project management team* are formally confirmed; which involves naming members of the *Project Board*, the *Project Manager* and any individuals required for assurance and support roles. Resources required to execute the *Initiation Stage Plan* are also committed.

Lastly, news of the approval is published to interested parties, and the *Project Manager* is given authorisation to kick off the *Initiation Stage*.

That's it for now for *Directing a Project*. The next scheduled activity – *authorise the project* – runs at the conclusion of the *Initiation Stage*, which is the subject of Chapter 6.

Summary

Pre-project establishes control for a PRINCE2 project and then subjects it to an initial test of its 'why?' credentials. The *Starting up a Project* process runs the analysis work and produces a *Project Brief* and *Initiation Stage Plan*.

PRINCE2 process-in-a-box – starting up a project

Purpose summary: to determine whether or not the project has sufficient merit to warrant proceeding to formal initiation

Trigger: Issue of a *project mandate* (by those responsible for commissioning projects)

Activities	Key management products

• *Appoint the Executive and the Project Manager*
 • *Capture previous lessons*
 • *Design and appoint the project management team*
 • *Prepare the outline Business Case*
 • *Select the project approach and assemble the Project Brief*
 • *Plan the Initiation Stage*
	• *Executive*
	 • *Project Manager*
	 • Remaining *project management team* (including *Project Board*)
	 • *Project Brief*; incorporating
	  – *Outline Business Case*
	  – *Project Product Description*
	 • *Initiation Stage Plan*
	 • *Daily Log*
	 • *Lessons Log*

End result: A *request to initiate a project* (where sufficient business justification exists) is submitted to the *Project Board*

Events kick off with the appointment of the *Executive* followed by the *Project Manager*. The rest of the *project management team* is then lined up for formal confirmation if the go-ahead is given.

Some high level work is needed to explore the requirements and to investigate delivery options. This is one input to the *Executive's* initial assessment of the business justification for the project. Meanwhile, the *Project Manager's* planning skills are put to use crafting a course of action for the *Initiation Stage*.

Directing a Project picks up the results and then drives the *Project Board* to abandon or move on a decision.

PRINCE2 process-in-a-box – directing a project

Purpose summary: to make key management decisions and to exercise overall project control

Triggers:

Request to initiate a project (initial trigger) from the *Project Manager* – or –

Request to deliver a project from the *Project Manager* – or –

Request to approve next Stage Plan from the *Project Manager* – or –

Request to approve Exception Plan from the *Project Manager* – or –

Project Manager request for advice – or –

Closure recommendation from the *Project Manager*

Activities	Key management products
● *Authorise Initiation* ● *Authorise the Project* ● *Authorise a Stage or Exception Plan* ● *Give ad hoc direction* ● *Authorise project closure*	● Approval of *Project Brief* and *Initiation Stage Plan* ● Approval of *Stage Plans* ● Approval of *Exception Reports* ● Advice and guidance ● Approval for project closure

End results:

Approval to initiate a project given to the *Project Manager*

Approval to move to the next stage given to the *Project Manager*

Approval to replace the current plan with an *Exception Plan*

Project Board advice and guidance supplied to *Project Manager*

Approval to close a project

Pre-project is carried out with an open and objective mind. It's readily accepted that a project that's abandoned after having been found to have a weak *Business Case* at modest cost, is as much of a success as one more promising that makes it through to initiation.

CHAPTER 5

Business case

Why, oh why?

PRINCE2 topic covered in this chapter:

- *Business Case theme*

The safest way to double your money is to fold it over and put it in your pocket.

Kin Hubbard (1868–1930)

Introduction

This is an excellent place at which to pause for a tour of PRINCE2's *Business Case* theme and its analysis techniques. They're put to good use at the next step: *Initiation Stage*. This is when the opening view of a project's justification is developed in detail, and then subjected to closer scrutiny.

PRINCE2 theme

The purpose of the *Business Case* theme is to establish mechanisms to judge whether the project is (and remains) desirable, viable and achievable as a means to support decision making in its (continued) investment.

Source: © Crown Copyright 2009. Cabinet Office.

The theme is an expansion upon the principle of *continued business justification*. In addition to advice on the initial preparation of a *Business Case*, there's an explanation of how this is then maintained and kept under review. Guidance is also given on benefits measurement, and the preparation of plans to track benefits delivery both during a project and after it has closed.

The approach advocated by PRINCE2 is based on a common method of making business decisions: evaluating the balance between costs, benefits and risks. For a project to run, the benefits must outweigh the costs involved and the risks that will be taken.

With a nod to PRINCE2's *product* focus, it's only right to start with the key deliverable: the *Business Case*.

What's in a business case?

A PRINCE2 project explains the rationale for its existence in a *Business Case* document. This records the reason for undertaking the venture, and acts as the ultimate reference point for all important project decisions. For example, if a call is needed on whether a *product* sits inside or outside of scope, or there's doubt about a requirement's priority, the impact on the *Business Case* is the yardstick used for arriving at the right conclusion.

The fundamentals of a PRINCE2 *Business Case* are:

- the reasons why the project is required;
- the recommended option for the meeting requirement, and why this is best;
- the expected costs and benefits, and key risks involved;
- taking into account the above, the overall value of the project.

All of the above need to be described in terms that its intended audience can understand, and presented in a way that's consistent with any established standards within the organisation.

 **example**

Business case – table of contents

A *Business Case* documents the business justification for a project. It would typically include the following sections:

Section	Typical contents
Executive Summary	A short (one page) summary of the business justification for the project; covering the recommended option and its costs, benefits and risks
Background	The background to the project and an overview of the analysis work conducted
Project Need	A description of why the project is needed, explaining how it's aligned to the overall strategy of the organisation
Recommended Option	A clear description of the business option being recommended and a summary of other discounted options, along with their relative merits and drawbacks. For the recommended option, the high level time-line for project and benefits delivery
Costs	An account of all of the resources (e.g. financial and people) that will be needed: (a) to deliver the project; and then (b) to operate and maintain its outputs over the period covered by the *Business Case*. A description of how the resources will be funded or obtained
Benefits	An assessment of the expected net benefit of the project. This includes identification of positive benefits and negative consequences (*dis-benefits*)
Risks	Identification of key risks to project delivery and benefits attainment; with estimates of their probabilities and impacts, and proposed mitigations
Investment Appraisal	An assessment of the value of the project through an analysis of costs, benefits and risks. A description of any factors which would have a significant impact on the analysis if they deviated from expectations. Objective conclusions as to the strength of the *Business Case*
Assumptions and Dependencies	A list of any significant assumptions that have been made during preparation of the *Business Case*, and identification of external dependencies

With the *Executive* taking overall responsibility, the *Business Case* is prepared in outline form during *Pre-project* and then developed in detail at *Initiation Stage*. It's subsequently kept up to date all the way through to closure.

The *Executive* has overall responsibility for the *Business Case*, with the *Senior User* owning the benefit descriptions. The analysis and authoring of the document can be delegated, for example, to a business analyst or the *Project Manager*. The *Project Assurance* team may also have some useful expertise to call upon, such as advice on financial appraisal techniques.

 **tip**

> Keep the *Executive* at less than arm's length from the *Business Case*. Use their knowledge of the audience to shape what's included and how this is presented. Ensure they're 100% bought into the final result too. Your lead salesperson needs to be convinced to be convincing!

Initial assessments of timescales, costs and risks are provided through the preparation of a *Project Plan* by the *Project Manager*. This exercise contributes information for the recommended option, and for the primary alternatives that have been discounted. A degree of iteration between the *Business Case* and *Project Plan* can be expected; as planning information helps to shape business alternatives, and refined options are reflected in the developing plan.

The planning process also adds to the list of assumptions and dependencies. Once the project is underway, data are regularly refreshed with actual values and revised forecasts.

Costs

The cost element of the *Business Case* equation extends to what's sometimes referred to as the 'total cost of ownership'. This goes beyond the initial implementation resources, and takes into account what it will take to keep what's delivered in use for some specified period of time (typically somewhere between three to five years).

This concept crops up in everyday life. Perhaps you've investigated printer options for your personal computer, and spotted that some manufacturers seem to offer a very attractive purchase price. Further research is required on the operating costs – ink and paper – before you can out if the apparent bargain is such a good investment after all. Maybe you're being enticed into a deal where the real costs only become apparent once the first replacement cartridge needs to be bought.

Benefits

Whereas costs tend to be relatively straightforward to describe, benefits can be more slippery customers. Not all can be expressed in terms of a neat financial return. Many projects are designed to provide a mix of financial and non-financial benefits, and some have no financial dimension at all. For example, investment in a road safety project will have some financial return, since dealing with the aftermath of an accident can be expensive. However, all would agree that preventing injury has important non-financial benefits, and these alone could be sufficient to justify a project. So techniques are required to allow all flavours of benefit to be described and compared.

PRINCE2 recognises that change introduced by a project usually has some downsides; even if this is simply the disruption caused during implementation. Whilst you may be excited about having that new kitchen fitted, you know you'll have to put up with microwave meals for a week whilst the work is carried out. These negative outcomes are known as *dis-benefits*. So that an accurate picture of the *net* benefit of the project can be drawn, *dis-benefits* are recorded in the *Business Case* alongside their more attractive cousins.

Risks

The third leg of the *Business Case* argument is risk. This deals with possible events that would negatively or positively impact costs and/or benefits. The assessment encompasses risks to delivery and to successful on-going operational use of the results.

The first port of call is the project's *Risk Register*. This source is also assessed during construction of plans, with identified threats and opportunities helping to shape the approach. This is an example of iteration between the planning process and development of the *Business Case*. For example, the cost of eliminating an adverse risk completely may prove prohibitive, and so some toing-and-froing would be required until the best compromise is found between level of investment and risk exposure.

The *Business Case* highlights the key threats to, and opportunities for, the forecast benefits at the price quoted. It also summarises the overall risk profile.

 **tip**

When presenting negative risks, in the same breath explain what's included in the plan to manage them. This inspires significantly more confidence in your audience than a simple list of what might go wrong.

Options, options, options

However good a *Business Case* is, it's still right to ask 'is there an even better one to be had?' Therefore, the development of a PRINCE2 *Business Case* involves searching out the options available, and weighing up their relative pros and cons. So even for a mandatory project, such as one to meet a legal requirement, the decision makers should push to see if there's a more cost-effective means of achieving the same result.

During the quest for the best value approach, the 'do nothing' option is always considered. This provides the costs and benefits accrued, and risks incurred if no action is taken. This is a baseline against which other options can be compared. It's also useful for highlighting the implications of inaction.

Organisations have finite resources, and so options *across* projects have to be considered as well. Therefore, to get the go-ahead a *Business Case* needs to demonstrate that it's a better value investment than its fellow contestants. This is addressed with an *investment appraisal*, which provides the data that are taken along to the beauty parade hosted by the corporate or programme management team.

Techniques for describing benefits

To be compelling, a *Business Case* has to be crystal clear about the benefits that it's claiming. It also has to have credibility. Experience shows that vague or unsubstantiated claims don't play well with senior managers, and are likely to result in a swift 'no thanks' in response.

PRINCE2 gives the job of describing benefits to the people who should be best placed to hit the mark: the people who'll specify and then use what the project will deliver. The *Senior User* holds overall responsibility for specifying the expected benefits. In addition, each benefit is assigned an owner, who is then accountable (along with the *Senior User*) for delivering the promised benefits. This accountability certainly focuses the mind and encourages realism.

brilliant tip

Looking for a way to tell your benefits story? Try summing up the achievements you're after with answers to the following questions:

- What's the current problem?
- What's going to be done about it?
- What's the intended outcome?
- How will that benefit us?

PRINCE2 recommends that all benefits are expressed in a way that's measurable; including those that are non-financial. Benefits which are quantifiable in monetary terms are relatively straightforward to describe; for example 'an increase in value of sales by 10%'. Other non-financial benefits can be quantified too, for example, 'halving the average number of accidents per month'.

Sometimes it can be challenging to produce practical direct measures. Imagine that a manufacturer wants to improve its factory's emergency evacuation plan. The expected benefit is a reduced probability of injury in the event of a catastrophe. Putting this into *direct* quantifiable terms would require detailed knowledge of how workers would respond to a whole range of emergency scenarios – both now and after the improved plan is implemented. This information is unlikely to be available, so it's reasonable to identify some *indirect* measures of benefit delivery. This might include demonstrating a 100% target of staff receiving improved emergency training within the previous 12 months, and evidence of successful evacuation exercises being run at least every 6 months.

To be of value as part of the **Business Case**, it must be practical to take an initial baseline measure and then to repeat this once the benefit is believed to be delivered. If this isn't feasible, there's no real point in including the claim since no one will ever know if it's been achieved.

 brilliant definition

Does a 'benefit' make it into the *Business Case*? Only if it is:

- **Quantified**: it incorporates a tangible measurement.
- **Measurable**: there's a practical way of measuring it – both before and after the project has delivered.
- **Owned**: someone appropriate has agreed to take responsibility for delivering it.
- **Linked to the project**: there is a clear connection with the project's outputs and the impact that these will have.
- **Linked to the organisation**: it's consistent with the wider aims and objectives of the organisation.

There should be a traceable link between a project's benefits and its *products*. This provides a handy cross-check. Every *product* needs to contribute to at least one benefit – either directly or indirectly – or it has no useful purpose. Similarly, it should be clear that each claimed benefit can be achieved through use of the proposed *products*. Understanding this relationship also helps future decision making; for example, when debating scope or assessing the impact of a fumbled *product* delivery.

 **tip**

Use the list of benefits to sharpen up your quality targets. If achieving a return demands a specific capability or feature, make sure this gets a specific mention in *Product Descriptions* and/or *acceptance criteria.*

Investment appraisal

If an overall value can be put on a project, the *Executive* is lent a hand when determining whether to proceed or to call a halt. These data also allow a like-with-like comparison between one proposal and another.

The source information needed to arrive at this value lies in the cost, benefit and risk analysis undertaken. There is a variety of investment-appraisal techniques for comparing total costs and net benefits, and for including a quantification of risk. PRINCE2 doesn't prescribe the techniques to use, and so these are selected based on the nature of the project and standards set by the organisation.

 **example**

Investment appraisal techniques

Here's a simple scenario to illustrate some metrics that can be used within a financial *Business Case.*

A project has implementation costs which will all be incurred in Year 1. From Year 2 the outputs are used and this turns a profit – albeit with an uplift in operating costs. This *Business Case* is being considered over a five-year timeframe.

	Year 1	Year 2	Year 3	Year 4	Year 5	Total
Implementation costs	10,000	–	–	–	–	10,000
Operating costs	–	2,000	1,000	1,000	1,000	5,000
Profit	–	1,000	3,000	8,000	9,000	21,000

Three metrics are calculated:

- **Net benefit** = the value of the benefits (profit) less implementation costs and increased operating costs.
- **Return on investment** = the profits expressed as a proportion of the costs (implementation and operating).
- **Payback period** = the time that will be required for the investment to break even.

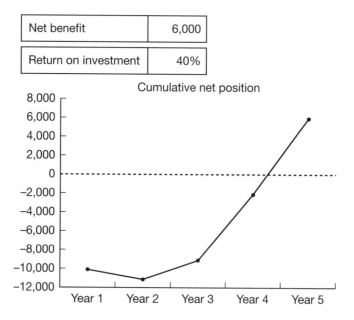

Net benefit	6,000
Return on investment	40%

In this example, there's a net profit over five years (6,000) and a healthy rate of return (40%). However, some investors might be put off by how long they'd have to wait to be up on the deal (more than four years).

The relative weight attached to costs, benefits and risks varies from one organisation to another. For example, if you're strapped for cash, a proposal that requires significant up-front investment will be a non-starter even when there's an attractive long-term prize to be won. The desired balance between these factors can also alter over time. So a change in fortune or an evolving attitude to risk might open up options that weren't previously on the table.

The cost and benefit figures plugged into the investment appraisal are only estimates. So what if they turn out to be wrong? This is a question addressed by a *sensitivity analysis*. This explores the impact that estimate variations have on the overall strength of the **Business Case**, and uncovers the factors that exert the biggest influence. Attention can then be focused on the relevant figures' level of accuracy and reliability. That way, the overall project value can be calculated for a range of credible scenarios, and any important health warnings attached.

A measure of success

The time and effort spent crafting benefit descriptions, constructing a **Business Case**, and weighing one option against another counts for little if this remains a purely academic exercise. Some hard data are called for if a project's true worth is to be established.

Consequently PRINCE2 insists that a **Business Case** is accompanied by a plan to track benefits delivery. The **Benefits Review Plan**, as it's known, explains how and when benefits will be measured and who's responsible for this.

There's one thorny issue to be cracked: most benefits for most projects are finally attained some time after closure. So there's a real risk of a **Business Case** being quietly forgotten once the team members have headed off in different directions. PRINCE2's solution is two-fold. First, the **Benefits Review Plan** sets out *all* of the required inspecting and reporting activities – not just those scheduled for the period when the project is still active.

Second, responsibilities are defined up-front to ensure that the benefits-tracking baton gets passed on as part of closure. These are assigned to a part of the organisation that represents a logical long-term choice for benefits assessment work. In fact, the duty could be taken on centrally from the outset. If not, the **Executive** initially starts off in the driving seat.

The **Business Case** analysis provides much of the information needed for the **Benefits Review Plan**. The practicalities of obtaining benefit measures are considered, and a decision is made as to when it's best to record the baseline and then to follow up. In recognition of the fact that benefits delivery is unlikely to pan out precisely as intended, some additional effort is budgeted for. This anticipates time to investigate the extra benefits and unforeseen drawbacks that pop up, and to unpick why these have occurred.

 **example**

Benefits review plan – table of contents

A **Benefits Review Plan** describes how and when the project's benefits will be measured. It is first prepared by the **Project Manager** during **Initiation Stage**, and would typically include the following sections:

Section	Typical contents
Background	The background to the project and the benefits that it is expected to deliver
Planned Benefits	An inventory of the benefits, with their owners and measures
Benefits Measurement Plan	How benefits are to be measured, when measurements will be taken, and the resources required. Includes arrangements for reporting results and handing over tracking responsibilities at project closure
Benefits Baseline	A set of measurements that provide a baseline against which the impact of the project can be evaluated

The **Benefits Review Plan** is maintained through the project with information on benefits delivered to date and revised forecasts of future benefit delivery.

It's recommended that the **Benefits Review Plan** is kept distinct from other plans, so that its activities can easily be separately managed.

Business case lifecycle

The **Business Case** is a thread that runs the full length of a project. Its lifecycle starts with the issuing of a **project mandate**. From there it runs all the way from initiation through to closure, and then on to final benefits delivery. PRINCE2 summarises the set of activities involved as:

- **Develop:** build the *Business Case* so that initiation and delivery go/no-go decisions can be made.
- **Maintain:** as delivery progresses, update the analysis with actual data and revised forecasts.
- **Verify:** formally revisit the *Business Case* at defined review points to assess whether or not a business justification still exists.
- **Confirm:** assess whether expected benefits have been achieved, and revise future benefit forecasts.

Business Case development spans *Pre-project* and *Initiation Stage*, resulting in the outline and detailed versions respectively. Once delivery is underway, the detailed *Business Case* is maintained with actual data and revised forecasts as they become available.

The *Project Board* verifies that the project is still worthwhile at all key decision points. This includes the checkpoints for moving to initiation and to delivery, and at each stage boundary. It's also an important consideration when new risks or issues are indentified and their impacts investigated.

brilliant tip

At all times a PRINCE2 project must be:

- **Desirable**: taking into account the estimated resources required and the risks involved, the expected benefits provide an attractive return.
- **Viable**: there's confidence that the project will deliver its *products*.
- **Achievable**: there's good reason to believe that if the delivery commitment is met, the promised benefits will be attained.

If at any time it doesn't meet these criteria, the project must be changed or stopped.

The *Executive* is ultimately accountable for ensuring that the project remains worthwhile. The assistance of the assurance function is enlisted to ensure the information on which this judgement is based is accurate.

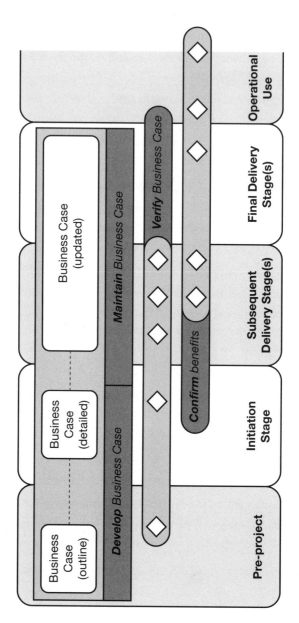

Figure 5.1 Business case lifecycle

At the end of each delivery stage, and adhering to the course of action set out in the *Benefits Review Plan*, benefits are **confirmed**. This entails:

- taking measures for those benefits which are due to be delivered;
- reconsidering the estimates for remaining benefits;
- making refinements (as required) to the plan.

Measurement will almost certainly have to run on beyond project closure, to allow for a full assessment to be made of the extent to which forecast benefits are achieved.

Summary

A *Business Case* is the driving force behind a PRINCE2 project, and it's used as the reference point for all major decisions. It summarises the outline justification for initiation, and then the detailed argument for advancing to delivery. As each stage concludes, and if circumstances change at any point, the *Business Case* either continues to stack up or the project is wound up.

With input from the *Project Plan*, the *Business Case* is built upon an assessment of costs, benefits and risks. A wide perspective is taken. *Dis-benefits* are added to the equation, and the analysis looks beyond implementation and ahead to operational use.

Making claims about future gains is fine, but achieving them is what really matters. PRINCE2 pushes for objective evidence to be produced. So the upsides have to be measurable – both before and after – to be included within the *Business Case*. Furthermore, a user representative is needed to endorse each benefit on the list. Finally, a *Benefits Review Plan* ensures that responsibilities for tracking the impact made aren't dropped post-closure.

 recap

- A PRINCE2 project records its business justification in a *Business Case* document.

- The *Executive* is accountable for the *Business Case*, with the *Senior User* taking overall responsibility for the definition and achievement of benefits.

- Develop, maintain, verify and confirm: a *Business Case* lifecycle runs for the duration and even beyond closure.

- To make the grade, benefits must be: quantified, measurable and owned.

- The *Benefits Review Plan* is where benefits measurement and reporting responsibilities are recorded.

CHAPTER 6

Initiation stage

Blueprints and foundations

PRINCE2 topics covered in this chapter:

- *Initiating a Project* process
- *Managing a Stage Boundary* process
- *Directing a Project* process – *Authorise the project*, and *Authorise a Stage or Exception Plan* activities

Before anything else, preparation is the key to success.

Alexander Graham Bell (1847–1922)

Introduction

One common cause of project failure is a lack of up-front preparation. This might be caused by the belief that there's no time to be wasted on luxuries such as planning or requirements analysis. Some are simply unable to resist the urge to get stuck in to the 'real' project work.

Fortunately, PRINCE2 comes to the aid of *Project Boards* and their *Project Managers*, by insisting that the right foundations are laid before the building work starts. This includes making the final call on whether the construction effort should indeed start in the first place.

PRINCE2 provides a dedicated process for this stage; the aptly titled *Initiating a Project*. This develops the detailed *Business Case* with its accompanying *Project Plan*. It also results in monitoring and control mechanisms being set up.

To complete the picture for *Initiation Stage*, this chapter also covers two more processes that come into play. First, there's the opening encounter with *Managing a Stage Boundary*. This takes care of the transition from initiation to the first delivery stage, and produces the detailed plan for the latter. Second, the *Directing a Project* story continues. PRINCE2 provides activities to cover the *Project Board* decisions to authorise the transition to delivery, and to approve the detailed plan for the first stage of work.

The processes of *Initiating a Project* and *Managing a Stage Boundary* make extensive use of PRINCE2's planning techniques, which are described in Chapter 7.

It shouldn't happen on a project (but did) . . .

In the days when the Internet revolution was dawning, a *Project Manager* found herself responsible for implementing an on-line payments system to tight deadlines. There was one *small* problem with the project requirements: the business was still busy re-designing itself and wasn't ready to reveal what it wanted. Sensing that time was running out, she decided to skip a couple of steps and to get her development team busy coding anyway.

The project ended up late regardless – but with huge wasted effort in the process. The team was left trying to unpick the car crash of what had been built on guesswork and what was really required.

The trick of saving time and effort by skipping the preparatory steps of a project is rarely pulled off. In fact the more likely outcome is a worse result than if the impossible deadlines or an unachievable price had been tackled upfront.

The logical place to start is with the process that lays the foundations: *Initiating a Project*.

Initiating a project

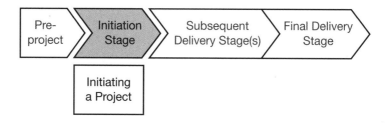

Having established that an idea for a project warrants serious consideration, the next step is to undertake the analysis work to support the final decision on whether or not to proceed with delivery. This decision is based upon the strength of a detailed *Business Case*. This in turn needs access to reliable information about what resources will be required, how long the work will take, and what level of risk is being taken on.

Objectives for initiating a project

- Ensuring that a detailed *Business Case* is established.
- Agreeing the scope of the project and what it will deliver.
- Preparing an overall *Project Plan* that includes estimates of the time and resources required.
- Establishing mechanisms for monitoring and controlling the work, and for assuring that delivery is fit for purpose.

The *Executive* has overall responsibility for development of the *Business Case*, with the *Project Manager* leading on planning work. Initiation is the point at which thought is given to management controls as well. So the *Project Manager* also picks up responsibility for defining and implementing mechanisms for managing risk, quality, change control, and project communications.

PRINCE2 defines the process using eight activities:

- *Prepare the Risk Management Strategy*
- *Prepare the Configuration Management Strategy*
- *Prepare the Quality Management Strategy*
- *Prepare the Communication Management Strategy*
- *Set up the Project Controls*
- *Create the Project Plan*
- *Refine the Business Case*
- *Assemble the Project Initiation Documentation.*

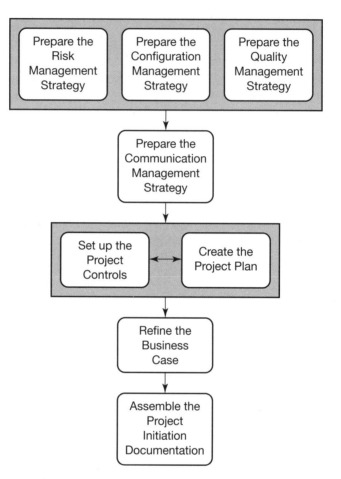

Figure 6.1 PRINCE2's recommended path through the activities of Initiating a Project
Source: Based on material from the PRINCE2 manual. © Crown Copyright 2009. Cabinet Office.

The key outputs from these activities are a detailed *Business Case, Benefits Review Plan, Project Plan,* and a set of management controls with their supporting registers. The papers produced are collected in a document set PRINCE2 calls *Project Initiation Documentation.*

Prepare the risk, configuration and quality management strategies

PRINCE2 advises setting up a range of management controls before launching into building a *Project Plan* and refining the *Business Case.* After all, this work needs properly managing too. The coverage of the controls includes:

- **Risk Management.** The procedures and techniques used to identify, assess and respond to project risks.

- **Configuration Management.** The procedures and techniques used to ensure change within the project is formally controlled, and that outputs are tracked.

- **Quality Management.** The procedures and techniques used to establish what constitutes a fit-for-purpose delivery, and to ensure this is then achieved.

The *Project Manager* is responsible for developing strategies for dealing with each of these management topics. PRINCE2 provides a sound starting point for all three areas via its *Risk, Change* and *Quality themes* (see Chapters 7 and 9). These all-purpose frameworks are tailored to reflect the specifics of the project at hand. This includes taking account of factors such as scale and complexity, and the anticipated level of risk involved.

 **action:** Good general questions to ask when setting management strategies

- What relevant standards and guidelines does the organisation have? How should these be incorporated within project controls?

- What do lessons learned reveal about the right project controls to have? For example, what does experience suggest is vital, and what only adds 'red tape'?

- What specific features of the project have a direct bearing on how risks, configuration and quality should be managed? The answers might include the number of people involved, the complexity of the delivery approach, or the implications of making a substandard delivery.

- Will project controls need approval from outside of the project; for example, from a central assurance function? If so, is there a benefit in some early involvement?

Whilst it's recognised that controls need to be tailored, PRINCE2's project management techniques do require that the following logs and records be set up and populated with initial data:

- *Risk Register* – for holding information about project risks.
- *Issue Register* – for maintaining information about issues that are being formally managed.
- *Configuration Item Records* – for tracking the status of *products*.
- *Quality Register* – for recording details of planned and actual quality activities.

The resulting *Risk, Configuration* and *Quality Management Strategies* are written up. Descriptions are provided of:

- procedures that will be followed, with the timing and frequency of key activities;
- roles and responsibilities;
- tools and techniques to be employed for analysing and responding to events;
- how assurance will be given that the management controls are operating as advertised;
- records to be kept.

The documents are added to the *Project Initiation Documentation* set, for approval by the *Project Board*.

Prepare the communication management strategy

Next comes the job of determining the *Communication Management Strategy* for the project. This specifies who needs what information, when they need it, who has the task of providing it, and how this will all happen.

Some of the information flows required can be extracted from the management strategies already developed. However, a much wider perspective is needed. This can be obtained through an analysis of the communication needs of all of the project's stakeholders.

Once it's designed, the *Project Manager* oversees the write up of the *Communication Management Strategy.* It's then included it in the *Project Initiation Documentation* set for approval by the *Project Board*.

Set up the project controls

Having worked on individual areas of management, it's time to establish an integrated set of project controls. These implement the level of supervision needed by the *Project Board*, and further down the management line between *Project Manager* and *Team Manager*.

Examples of key controls are:

* the number of stages that the project is broken into, providing a formal checkpoint between each one;
* the limits that are placed on delegated authorities, and the mechanisms set up to monitor the project's current and forecast position against these;
* procedures for handling exceptions to the plan.

Many of the mechanisms will already have been defined within the *Risk, Configuration* and *Quality Management Strategies*. These are brought together, with the objective of filling any gaps and ensuring that a set of integrated controls is in place. The *Project Manager* is responsible for documenting the results, and for ensuring that responsibilities are reflected in the team structure and associated role descriptions.

Create the project plan

In order to refine the *Business Case* – and so reach a decision on taking the project further – reliable answers are needed to a couple of vital questions: 'how much?' and 'how long?'. This calls for a delivery plan to be drawn up. This exercise provides additional insight into another important dimension of the *Business Case*: the risks involved. It also provides the *Project Board* with a baseline against which the performance of the project can be measured.

Starting with the *Project Brief* created during *Pre-project*, and working with customer and supplier representatives, the *Project Manager's* task is to prepare a plan to cover the whole project. This is only required down to the level of detail demanded by the *Business Case* – the preparation of plans to manage on a day-to-day basis comes later. However, to get an accurate picture of the totality of what's needed, the plan does need to extend beyond the core deliverables. So allowance is made for management and control activities, such as those for assurance, reporting and communications. Consideration is also given to the tasks required to put an appropriate support service in place – either as an extension to an existing organisation or as something that needs to be built from the ground up.

 example

Project plan – table of contents

A *Project Plan* describes the plan for the end-to-end project and is used by the *Project Board* as a baseline for measuring progress. It's first prepared by the *Project Manager* during *Initiation Stage*, and would typically include the following sections:

Section	Typical contents
Background	The background to the project and a summary of progress made to date
Plan Overview	A summary of the purpose of the *Project Plan*, what it includes, the approach taken to developing it, and any important lessons that have been incorporated. A high level description of the plan and its management stages
Project Budgets and Tolerances	The time and resource budgets to be allocated for the project. Project level tolerances set for scope, time and resources
Products	Identification of the project's major *products*, possibly supported by a *product breakdown structure* and/or a *product flow diagram*. A set of *Product Descriptions* for each *product* listed
Project Schedule	A graphical representation of the project schedule (e.g. as a Gantt chart) at summary level, with a list of key project milestones
Resources Needed	A summary schedule of the resources needed to deliver the project, including people resources (identified by name or by role)
Project Controls	A description of the procedures that will be used to manage the plan and to monitor performance
Assumptions and Dependencies	A list of any significant assumptions that have been made during preparation of the plan, and identification of external dependencies

The *Project Plan* is maintained throughout the project to reflect actual progress and revised forecasts.

Using PRINCE2's planning techniques, the project's major *products* are identified, described and analysed. This allows the necessary high level activities to be scoped and resources estimated. Development of the plan requires resolution of any significant issues, and it also provides a good opportunity to reflect on risks.

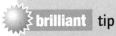 **tip**

Once resource needs have been identified, it's a case of 'book early to avoid disappointment'. Don't delay in confirming that key players are available and prepared to be committed to the project.

The *Project Manager* presents the outputs of the planning exercise in a *Project Plan* document. It's possible that the overall *Project Product Description* created during *Pre-project* needs to be refined to keep it in line with the greater understanding gained.

Refine the business case

Once the estimates for project costs and timescales have been produced, work on the detailed *Business Case* can be completed. The resulting document lays out the benefits expected from the project; and puts these up against the resources that will be required, and the risks involved. It also presents any important timing considerations. For example, the pitch for your extravagant New Year's Eve party would be dealt a fatal blow if a suitable venue couldn't be secured until the second of January.

The *Executive* ensures that the *Business Case* is sufficiently robust to drive the decision whether or not the project should be delivered. Tolerances are also set for the expected benefits. These are designed to provide a trigger for re-visiting the business justification in circumstances where the rationale for the project is thrown into doubt.

Lastly, the *Project Manager* produces the *Benefits Review Plan* to record how benefits will be measured, and who has responsibility tracking and reporting on them.

Assemble the project initiation documentation

By this point, a lot of preparatory work has been invested in to guide the decision about proceeding further. The final step is to collate the results within the *Project Initiation Documentation* set. This will be used to gain approval for the project.

Project Initiation Documentation inventory:

- *Business Case*
- *Project Plan*
- *Product Descriptions*
- *Project management team structure*
- *Role descriptions*
- *Risk Management Strategy*
- *Configuration Management Strategy*
- *Quality Management Strategy*
- *Communication Management Strategy*
- *Project Controls*

Rather than trying to shoe-horn everything into a single tome, the *Project Initiation Documentation* is typically a collection of documents. A pragmatic decision is taken on how to package up the analysis; based upon factors such as the size of the project, and the groups of people working on the various aspects of initiation.

It's important that the exact configuration of documents submitted is preserved. This baseline allows future decisions to be made with reference to the basis on which the project was originally authorised. It also allows deviations from the original *Business Case* and *Project Plan* to be tracked.

Completion of this final activity runs in parallel with the *Managing a Stage Boundary* process, which provides the detailed plan for the first delivery stage. When this is ready, a request to deliver the project is submitted to the *Project Board*.

Managing a stage boundary

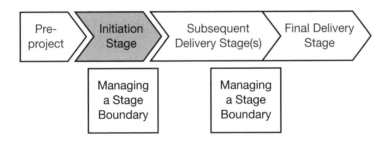

PRINCE2's *Managing a Stage Boundary* process provides the *glue* between stages. It's used when making the transition between the *Initiation Stage* and first delivery stage, and between further delivery stages (where multiple stages are being used). The process is also called into action on an ad hoc basis when tolerances are forecast to be exceeded. The *Project Board* can ask for an *Exception Plan* to be prepared, and this immediately brings the curtain down on the current stage. (A detailed account of escalation processes can be found in Chapter 8.)

Objectives for managing a stage boundary

- Assessing the completeness of the current stage.
- Providing the information needed to confirm that the project is still worthwhile and has a viable plan.
- Preparing a comprehensive plan for the next stage (or a replacement plan for the current stage if the wheels have fallen off).
- Requesting authorisation to proceed to the next stage or to adopt the *Exception Plan.*

Managing a Stage Boundary creates a detailed plan for the next stage, and ensures that the *Project Plan* and *Business Case* are kept in line. It consists of five activities:

- *Plan the next stage*
- *Produce an Exception Plan*
- *Update the Project Plan*
- *Update the Business Case*
- *Report stage end.*

The key outputs from these activities are a *Stage* or *Exception Plan*, updated *Project Plan* and *Business Case*, and *End Stage Report*. The latter is prepared by the *Project Manager* to summarise the current position and future outlook.

Plan the next stage

As the *Initiation Stage* nears its end, a detailed plan for the first (or perhaps only) delivery stage needs to be constructed. This will ultimately be submitted to the *Project Board* as part of seeking approval to move on. This process is repeated for subsequent delivery stages until the *Final Delivery Stage* is reached.

The *Project Plan* specifies what high level **products** apply to the next stage, and so provides the scope of what now needs to be mapped out in detail. If the approaching stage is the final one, this will include the necessary closure deliverables.

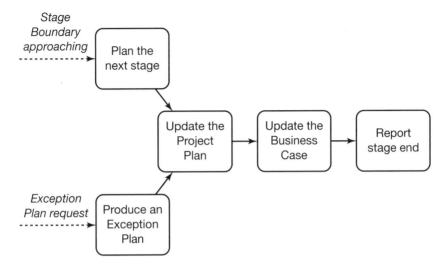

Figure 6.2 PRINCE2's recommended path through the activities of Managing a Stage Boundary

The stage planning process uses the same PRINCE2 planning techniques as those used to design the overall project. This time the exercise is taken down to the level of detail needed by the *Project Manager* to oversee work on a day-to-day basis. The summary *products* are broken down to give a complete list of all of the next stage's outputs. The planning cycle is then kicked off.

 **example**

Stage plan – table of contents

The contents of a *Stage Plan* are similar to those in the *Project Plan*, and would typically include the following sections:

Section	Typical contents
Background	The background to the project, a description of its stages, and a summary of progress made to date
Plan Overview	A summary of the purpose of the *Stage Plan*, what it includes, the approach taken to developing it, and any important lessons that have been incorporated. A high level description of the stage and the proposed approach

Section	Typical contents
Stage Budgets and Tolerances	The time and resource budgets to be allocated for the stage. Stage level tolerances set for scope, time and resources
Products	Identification of all of the stage's **products**, possibly supported by a **product breakdown structure** and/or a product flow diagram. A set of **Product Descriptions** for each **product** listed
Stage Schedule	A graphical representation of the stage schedule (e.g. as a Gantt chart), with a list of key milestones
Resources Needed	A schedule of the resources needed to deliver the stage, including people resources (identified by name or by role)
Project Controls	A description of the procedures that will be used to manage the plan and to monitor performance (e.g. through cross-referencing those specified in the **Project Plan**)
Assumptions and Dependencies	A list of any significant assumptions that have been made during preparation of the **Stage Plan**, and identification of external dependencies

The planning process results in updates to the **Risk, Issue** and **Quality Registers**. The comprehensive **product** inventory also contributes to the records being used to track the configuration of outputs.

The results are presented in a **Stage Plan**. This document is submitted to the **Project Board** when approval to move to the next stage is asked for.

Produce an exception plan

In a situation where a stage or the overall project is forecast to exceed tolerances, the **Project Board** may decide to commission an **Exception Plan**. This request effectively forces an early stage boundary. If approved, the **Exception Plan** replaces the current plan; allowing a new baseline to be set.

An **Exception Report** will already have been prepared to analyse the situation. This explains the deviation and its causes, and recommends a course of action. Using this and the existing **Stage Plan** as a starting point, a revised plan is developed. The resulting **Exception Plan** is submitted to the **Project Board** for approval.

 **tip**

Ensure lessons *really are* learned when an *Exception Plan* is required. It's an opportunity to create a positive out of a negative. In particular, a useful wake-up call is there to be exploited where wild optimism and wishful thinking are found to lie behind the failure of the previous plan.

Update the project plan

Once detailed planning is complete, it's time to look at how this impacts the overall project. The higher level *Project Plan* is adjusted so it's in line with the *Stage* or *Exception Plan* just prepared. It's also an opportunity to ensure that the *Project Plan* accurately reflects the actual progress that's been made. Other supporting documentation and records may need to be updated too. For example, if the planning work has mitigated some risks and identified others, the corresponding changes are made in the *Risk Register*.

Update the business case

An important objective of the *Managing a Stage Boundary* process is to ensure that the *Project Board* has the information it needs to confirm (or otherwise) that the project still has a sound business justification. This requires a re-visit of the fundamentals of the *Business Case*; i.e. costs, benefits and risks. These are re-examined in the light of any new information thrown up by the planning exercise.

The analysis isn't just inward looking. An assessment is also made of any external factors that could have a bearing on the *Business Case*. It's possible that events in the outside world have impacted costs, risks or benefits – or all three. The organisation might even have changed its mind about what constitutes an acceptable *Business Case*.

When a project is in the process of being initiated, and the detailed *Business Case* has only just been written, there should be little to do here. However, during later stages, events inside and outside of the project might force a re-think.

 **tip**

Continue or cancel? Some good questions to ask

- What does actual performance against the plan tell us about the reliability of cost and timing estimates for future work? If we maintain the current rate of progress, does the *Business Case* still stack up?

- Is the *Business Case* reliant on hitting key delivery dates? If so, are we still confident of meeting these?

- With what we now know about the solution we'll get, do the forecast benefits still look realistic?

- Have we uncovered any significant new costs, downsides or risks?

- Have any events outside of the project called the *Business Case* into question?

Where an *Exception Plan* has been prepared, the *Business Case* deserves a thorough review. Since agreed tolerances were on their way to be exceeded, determining if this has dealt a fatal blow to the original justification represents a sensible line of investigation.

The analysis may result in the need to revise the *Business Case* document. It's also possible that assessment of benefits delivered, or the revised view of those expected, requires an update to the *Benefits Review Plan*.

Report stage end

In preparation for a *Project Board* decision on the next action for the project, the revised documentation is assembled for review. It may also be useful to prepare a *Lessons Report* to summarise what has been learned to date. Entries in the *Lessons Log* provide much of the input.

The *Project Manager* is then responsible for producing an *End Stage Report*, which includes:

- an account of what the stage has delivered against that planned;

- an evaluation of performance against the plan;

- an assessment of the on-going viability of the overall *Project Plan*, supported by an identification of significant risks and issues;

- a view on the prospects for achieving the *Business Case*;
- any important lessons that have been learned.

There are a number of information sources for the report. These include the latest version of the *Business Case* and the *Benefits Review Plan*. A *Product Status Account* report from *Project Support* also provides a picture of progress made against the *products* falling within the scope of the stage; with a record of planned and actual performance.

In the situation where an *Exception Plan* has been requested, and based on how far through the current stage this was called for, the *Project Board* will determine if an *End Stage Report* is required alongside the plan.

 **example**

End stage report – table of contents

The *End Stage Report* presents the stage's performance against its agreed baseline(s), and summarises the overall project position. It's prepared by the *Project Manager* and typically includes the following sections:

Section	Typical contents
Executive Summary	A short (one page) summary of the performance of the stage against the objectives that were set for it, and the outlook for the next stage and overall project
Background	The context for the stage, its primary objectives and a brief narrative of events. An explanation of any changes that were approved to the starting baseline
Stage Performance	An account of the stage's performance against the targets and tolerances set for it; including resources, timescales, quality and scope
Product Delivery	A table of the principle planned *products*, confirming delivery (as appropriate) and with notes of any significant deviations from agreed requirements. A detailed log of all *products* and references to quality management records can be attached as an appendix
Follow-on Actions	If required, for handed-over *products*, a list of the actions needed to resolve outstanding issues and risks
Project Position	A review of where the overall project now stands in relation to the validity of its *Business Case* and performance against objectives. A summary of current issues and risks

Section	Typical contents
Outlook	A forecast for the project and next stage against planned targets and tolerances
Lessons Summary	A summary of important lessons learned, with a reference to any supporting **Lessons Report**
Follow-up Actions	A list of any actions, with owners, that are needed in connection with handed-over **products**

For a project that still appears viable, the **Project Manager** requests approval of the next **Stage Plan** or **Exception Plan**, and supporting documentation. At the **Initiation Stage**, this is submitted in parallel with the request to proceed with delivery.

Directing a project – act two

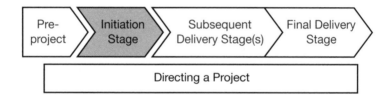

The **Directing a Project** process's initial objective was to authorise only those projects whose **Business Case** looked sufficiently promising to invest in a more detailed look. Once this analysis has been completed, the **Project Board** is then accountable for two further approvals. The first is to decide if the project should proceed to delivery or instead be halted. If the thumbs-up is given, the second verdict is whether or not to approve the detailed plan for the first delivery stage. This would then allow the project to make the transition from initiation to delivery.

These decisions are arrived at through two **Directing a Project** activities:

- *Authorise the project.*
- *Authorise a Stage or Exception Plan.*

The approval to move to delivery is given only once, at the conclusion of initiation. However, a call on whether or not to authorise the next stage is required at each stage boundary. This decision point applies to an *Exception Plan* too, since an exception brings the current stage to a premature end.

Authorise the project

A verdict on whether to allow a project to proceed to delivery is based on a *Project Board* review of the *Project Initiation Documentation* that has been assembled. The project's detailed *Business Case* and its supporting *Project Plan* contain the key information. The *Board* also reviews the *Benefits Review Plan*.

Project Board criteria for authorising a project:

- Does the project have a robust and viable *Business Case*?
- Is there a credible *Project Plan* for delivering what's needed to meet the *Business Case*?
- Will the proposed management strategies and project controls create an environment for effective and efficient delivery?
- Is it clear how the benefits will be measured, and is there a plan for doing this?

If the *Project Board* decides that a project should go ahead, the *Project Initiation Documentation* and *Benefits Review Plan* are signed off. The *Board* is responsible for securing the resources required for the whole project. These will then be released to the *Project Manager* on a stage-by-stage basis.

If the project hasn't made the grade, it's wound up using the *Closing a Project* process (see Chapter 10).

The activity to authorise a project runs in parallel with approval of the first delivery *Stage Plan*. The latter has to be agreed before the project can move on from initiation.

Authorise a stage or exception plan

The tasks to authorise the next stage involve both a look back and a look forward. The *End Stage Report* issued by the *Project Manager* provides a summary of the performance to date, and an assessment of the on-going viability of the *Business Case* and *Project Plan*. So approval of the plan for the next stage of work (*Stage Plan* or *Exception Plan*) is made in the context of performance to date, and with visibility of the current strength of the *Business Case*.

First, the *Project Board* needs to satisfy itself that the current management stage is complete. This includes verifying that all of the planned *products* have been delivered, and hand-overs made where necessary. Next the *Stage* or *Exception Plan* is reviewed to ensure that it meets the project need and is achievable. Any updates to the *Project Plan* are checked too. Before reaching a decision, the *Project Board* re-visits the *Business Case* to consider the on-going viability of the project.

brilliant tip

A stage boundary is just the right place to make full use of the *Project Assurance* function. Some independent expertise, and a fresh pair of eyes, provide useful insight when making the critical decision on whether the project is really ready to move on.

If approval is given, the *Project Manager* is authorised to proceed, and the necessary resources are committed. Alternatively, the *Board* may decide that the *Project Manager* needs to revise the plan. Where this is the case, the plan is rejected and guidance is given on the improvements required.

It's also possible that a decision is made to call a halt completely; for example, where detailed planning for the next piece of work has revealed that important assumptions underpinning the *Business Case* are flawed. When this kind of bad news is uncovered, the *Project Manager* is asked to close the project.

Summary

The *Initiation Stage* is where the foundations for a successful project are laid. The *Business Case* is developed in detail, and then scrutinised to ensure that construction work only begins where the venture is both worthwhile and achievable. This critical decision can only be made with access to a solid *Project Plan*. This isn't defined in copious low-level detail, but it does encompass everything that needs to be delivered.

Before the go-ahead can be given, a detailed plan is also required for the first delivery stage. This will be used by the *Project Manager* to oversee work on a day-to-day basis.

For *Initiation Stage*, PRINCE2's *Initiating a Project* process handles most of the groundwork. It sets up the necessary projects controls, creates the *Project Plan* and refines the *Business Case*. The results of the analysis are packaged up for the *Project Board* in a *Project Initiation Documentation* set. A *Benefits Review Plan* is also prepared to explain how the forecast benefits are to be measured and reported on.

PRINCE2 process-in-a-box – initiating a project

Purpose summary: to lay the groundwork for a successful project, and to provide the information required for an informed decision whether or not to proceed to delivery

Trigger: the *Authority to initiate project* is received from the *Project Board*

Activities	Key management products
<ul><li>*Prepare the Risk Management Strategy*</li><li>*Prepare the Configuration Management Strategy*</li><li>*Prepare the Quality Management Strategy*</li><li>*Prepare the Communication Management Strategy*</li><li>*Set up the Project Controls*</li><li>*Create the Project Plan*</li><li>*Refine the Business Case*</li><li>*Assemble the Project Initiation Documentation*</li></ul>	<ul><li>*Project Initiation Documentation* including:<ul><li>*Risk Management Strategy*</li><li>*Configuration Management Strategy*</li><li>*Quality Management Strategy*</li><li>*Communication Management Strategy*</li><li>*Project Controls*</li><li>*Project Plan*</li><li>*Product Descriptions*</li><li>*Detailed Business Case*</li></ul></li><li>*Benefits Review Plan*</li><li>*Risk Register*</li><li>*Configuration Item Records*</li><li>*Issue Register*</li><li>*Quality Register*</li></ul>

End results:

Request to deliver a project (where sufficient business justification exists)

Trigger to start detailed preparation for the next stage

As the *Initiation Stage* draws to a close, a project goes through its first formal transition from one *management stage* to the next. The *Managing a Stage Boundary* process handles the detailed preparation for the following stage, ensuring that the *Project Plan* and *Business Case* are refined as needed.

This process runs every time a new delivery stage approaches, and also in response to a request for an *Exception Plan*.

PRINCE2 process-in-a-box – managing a stage boundary

Purpose summary: to give the *Project Board* the information it needs to decide whether or not to approve: progress to the next stage, or the adoption of an *Exception Plan*

Triggers:

A stage status review identifies that a stage boundary is approaching – or –

An *Exception Plan* request is received from the *Project Board*

Activities	Key management products
● *Plan the next stage* ● *Produce an Exception Plan* ● *Update the Project Plan* ● *Update the Business Case* ● *Report stage end*	● *Stage Plan* for next stage – or – *Exception Plan* ● *Product Descriptions* ● Updated *Project Plan* ● Updated *Business Case* ● *Lessons Report* (if appropriate) ● *Product Status Account* ● *End Stage Report*

End result: a request to approve either the next *Stage Plan* for the next stage or an *Exception Plan*

Directing a Project continues to guide *Project Board* decision making. There's a one-off approval needed to authorise a project's delivery. As required when any new delivery stage is reached, a judgement is also given on the proposed next *Stage Plan*. Where an *Exception Plan* has been requested, this has to be signed-off from the *Project Board* before it can replace the current plan.

CHAPTER 7

Plans, quality and risk

Prepare to take control

PRINCE2 topics covered in this chapter:

- *Plans theme*
- *Quality theme*
- *Risk theme*

A lot of people approach risk as if it's the enemy when it's really fortune's accomplice.

Sting (1951–)

Introduction

By the completion of *Initiation Stage*, there's a detailed *Business Case* and a couple of related plans: the *Project Plan* and a *Stage Plan*. In fact, there's a third plan when you look a bit closer: the *Benefits Review Plan*. (Let's hope there's been no cause to call on an *Exception Plan* so early on!)

PRINCE2's approach to the *Business Case* was toured in Chapter 5, but how do all of these plans get built? PRINCE2's answer to this question lies within the three *themes* covered by this chapter:

- *Plans*
- *Quality*
- *Risk*

With the name *Plans*, there are no prizes for guessing that this is where fundamental planning techniques are laid out. There's also a run through of the types of plans PRINCE2 employs, and an explanation of how they all fit together.

There's a very close relationship between PRINCE2's approach to planning and to quality. In fact, in many ways they're two sides of the same coin. The *Quality* theme expands on how the *product*-based approach is used to prepare the project for a fit-for-purpose delivery.

Dealing with uncertainty is a topic that runs through both the *Business Case* and *Plans* themes. The *Risk* theme explains how to evaluate threats and opportunities so that they can be incorporated within the business justification. It also describes how the results of this analysis help to shape supporting delivery plans.

The plans theme

It would be an impressive feat to control a project without a plan. For example, how would you know what's next on the to-do list, whether you're ahead or behind, or even if you've finished? The cost and risk side of the *Business Case* equation would certainly be shrouded in mystery too. So it's no surprise that PRINCE2 has plenty to say about plans and planning.

PRINCE2 theme

The purpose of the *Plans* theme is to facilitate communication and control by defining the means of delivering the products (the where and how, by whom, and estimating the when and how much).

Source: © Crown Copyright 2009. Cabinet Office.

For PRINCE2 a plan is rightly much more than a timing schedule. A timetable of activities (or maybe *products*) is certainly important, but it's only part of the story. A plan also explains the objectives to be met, lists what's inside and outside of scope, specifies the deliverables, and describes what resources are needed. It inspires confidence that the targets it sets are achievable, and helps the players to understand what will happen and how they'll be involved.

Planning is an activity that requires effort and careful thought. However, it's the best investment a project can make. Within PRINCE2, it's also not optional. Its processes ensure that any temptation to skip the preparatory steps is swiftly overcome.

What planning brings to the party (beyond delivering a plan of action):

- clarity over exactly what needs to be delivered;
- driving out uncertainty, omissions, inconsistencies and unrealistic expectations by engaging the *project management team* and important stakeholders;
- building commitment to a common goal and how this is to be achieved;
- a baseline against which measures can be taken of progress and forecasts made of future performance.

A plan for all occasions

In PRINCE2's world there are five kinds of plan. The first two reflect the tactic of only planning to a level of detail that makes sense for the point you've reached. So, from the point of initiation, a project has:

- A **Project Plan** for the whole project. This provides an end-to-end summary plan. It's created during the *Initiation Stage*, and then maintained as the project progresses.
- A **Stage Plan** for the current stage. This is specified at the level of detail required by the *Project Manager* to supervise on a day-to-day basis. The plan for the next stage is always prepared as the current one draws to a conclusion. So the *Initiation Stage Plan* is prepared as part of *Starting up a Project*, and subsequent *Stage Plans* are developed each time a stage boundary approaches.

The third type of plan is an *Exception Plan*. This is produced when a venture goes off the rails, or – as PRINCE2 would say – when a project or stage is forecast to exceed its tolerances. The *Exception Plan* is designed to replace the plan that's in trouble. So, once approved, it becomes the new baselined *Project Plan* or *Stage Plan*.

Sometimes *products* within a stage are packaged up and handed out to smaller work teams to execute. In this case the responsible *Team Manager* may elect to develop a fourth kind of PRINCE2 plan: a *Team Plan*. PRINCE2 doesn't prescribe the format for a *Team Plan*, and so this takes the form of whatever suits the *Team Manager* – perhaps with some consultation with the *Project Manager*.

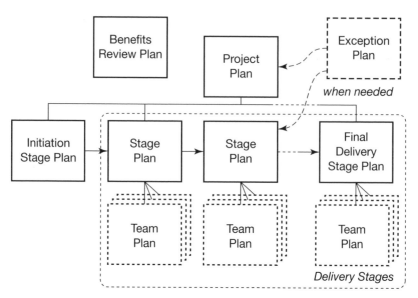

Figure 7.1 Hierarchy of PRINCE2 plans

The fifth, and final, type of plan is one that sits outside of the hierarchy spanning big picture through to fine detail. This is the **Benefits Review Plan**. It describes how and when benefits will be measured, and is independent of delivery plans.

The PRINCE2 planning process

PRINCE2 offers a common set of planning techniques that can be applied to any type of plan. As you might expect, its approach is heavily influenced by its principle of **focus on products**. In fact, its mandated **product**-based technique is a defining feature. It involves starting with what's going to be delivered before sorting out how this is to be achieved. Continuing with the enthusiasm for things coming in sevens, the following steps are involved:

1 **Design the plan.** Select the right planning tools and techniques, and decide how the plan will be presented.

2 **Define and analyse the products.** Agree the outputs and establish the relationship between them.

3 **Identify activities and dependencies.** List the necessary tasks and their dependencies.

4 **Prepare estimates.** Work out how long tasks will take and what resources they'll need.

5   **Prepare the schedule.** Develop a timeline supported by a credible resourcing plan.

6   **Analyse the risks.** Throughout the process, evaluate risks and adjust the plan where necessary.

7   **Document the plan.** Write up the results.

The second step, which scrutinises the plan's *products*, underpins the whole approach. It's broken down further to guide the process for cataloguing *products*, describing them and analysing their interrelationships.

Design the plan

The first step is to select the right planning tools and techniques. This includes making a decision on the level down to which the approach will be mapped out, and the estimating methods to be employed. Consideration also needs to be given to the intended audience for the plan, and how this should influence its presentation.

brilliant tip

Computerised planning tools ease the administrative overhead of building and maintaining plans. They also provide useful automated checks and balances. But never let the software take the lead. The *project management team* must understand and own the results of a planning exercise.

Some decisions on the plan design may already have been set by the organisation's standards. The same is likely to be true if the project is part of a wider programme of work. Such guidelines would provide the starting point for agreeing the approach.

Define and analyse the products

Now the planning proper starts. Where a *Project Plan* is being started, the first task is to write the *Project Product Description*. This is produced during initial scoping and refined through the *Initiating a Project* process. Then, for all plans:

●   a *product breakdown structure* is created;

●   *Product Descriptions* are written; and then

●   a *product flow diagram* is developed.

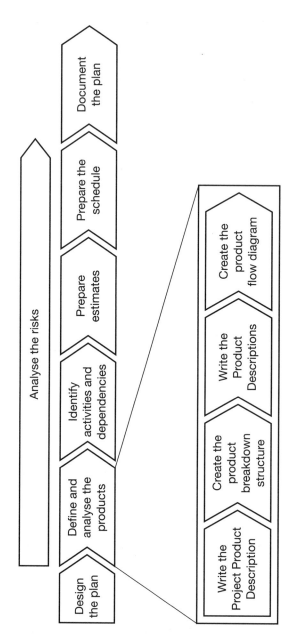

Figure 7.2 The PRINCE2 planning approach

The starting point is to break the plan down into its major *products*. Each *product* is itself then broken into its components parts. This process is repeated until the project's outputs are recorded at a level of detail that's consistent with the plan under development.

To provide a head start, and to encourage consistency, some organisations hold a library of standard *products*. When using such a resource it's important to avoid a copy-and-paste trap. The planning team needs to be confident that it has ended up with the right *product* list, and that it understands exactly how everything fits together.

brilliant tips for creating a product breakdown structure

- It's a creative process. Running an up-beat interactive workshop with a good mix of participants will give a better result than staring at a computer screen.
- There are many ways of slicing and dicing the *product* breakdown. Look for one that both (a) makes sense to those providing the input; and (b) gives a useful structure to the plan.
- Don't worry – you *will* know when to stop. Common sense calls a halt when the right level of detail is reached.
- A little bit of colour aids digestion; for example to illustrate whose responsible for which *products*.
- Use the exercise as a great opportunity to promote collaborative working and to ensure everyone's views are represented up-front.

It's useful to include any external *products* within the analysis. These are *products* that are needed by the project, but which exist already or are being created elsewhere. Their inclusion provides a fully rounded picture of project delivery.

The resulting *product breakdown structure* can be presented as a tree structure, showing the successive levels of detail.

 example

A simple product breakdown structure

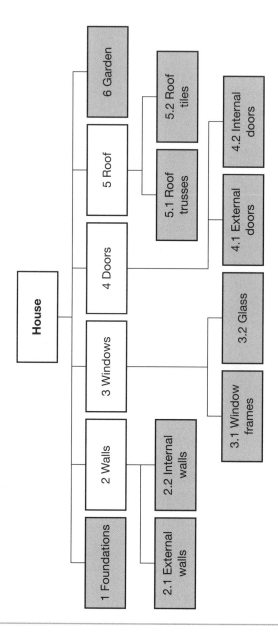

Once the plan's *products* have been identified, the process of describing these begins. A *Product Description* is written for each deliverable. This is likely to be an iterative process, with benefit to be gained from capturing an outline as soon as possible rather than waiting until a perfect specification can be crafted. *Production Descriptions* can then be refined as planning progresses, and there's a better understanding of exactly what's needed.

The preparation of *Product Descriptions* offers another great chance to get the team and other stakeholders involved. In particular, involving customer and supplier representatives makes a real contribution to a shared understanding of what has to be delivered. For example, it's an excellent opportunity to hone the *quality criteria* that record what constitutes a fit-for-purpose delivery.

brilliant tip

Stuck for inspiration? Get hold of *Product Descriptions* from other projects. There will be material that can be adapted, and some text that's directly re-usable. Making sense of someone else's efforts also provides some useful pointers on how to write *Product Descriptions* with clarity.

Once a plan approaches the point of being signed-off, the *Product Descriptions* falling within the scope of delivery get baselined. They're then subject to formal change control, and their maintenance forms part of the process for agreeing and documenting any later adjustments.

Having identified a plan's deliverables and written descriptions for them, the final *product* analysis step is to create a *product flow diagram*. This enables the dependencies between *products* to be explored and then presented graphically. Understanding these relationships is critical to constructing a realistic work plan. It sets out the order in which work should be tackled, highlighting what must be sequential and what could be run in parallel.

 example

A simple product flow diagram

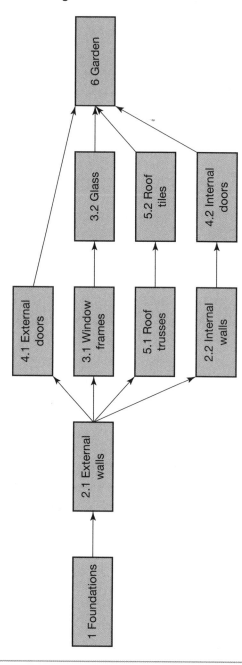

The *product flow diagram* lays out the *products* in sequence order, with lines connecting them to show dependencies. *External products* are included to provide the complete picture. Start and end markers are added if it's not immediately clear which *products* can be worked on first, and which is the last one to be completed.

Identify activities and dependencies

For most projects it's necessary to plan the activities for delivering *products*, rather than simply to work directly from the *product* analysis. However, with all the thought that's been invested in defining and analysing the plan's deliverables, working out what activities are required should be relatively straightforward.

The *product breakdown structure* and *product flow diagram* each provides a helpful starting point for developing the inventory of activities. It's important to achieve a complete coverage, and this extends to management and quality-related tasks. Work relating to external *products* is also captured, for example, to allow for receiving and checking a delivery from a third party.

Building on the analysis of dependencies between *products*, the relationships between activities are established too. So for example, work on constructing the roof on a house can't start until the supporting walls have been built. Some activity dependencies may be external, for example receiving approval to commence building works or taking a delivery of bricks ahead of construction.

Prepare estimates

Before a schedule can be put together, time and resource estimates are needed for each component piece of work. First resource requirements are identified. These might detail the different types of people, funding and equipment to be employed. For each category, an estimate is made of how much will be consumed to complete the task. By making some realistic assumptions about resource availability, a first stab can then be made at the elapsed time that should be allocated.

brilliant tip

Be on the look out for resources that are in short supply. These will place constraints on the plan. Their early identification provides the best chance to secure what's essential and to find ways of mitigating bottlenecks.

There are many ways of arriving at estimates and PRINCE2 doesn't advocate a particular approach. The best techniques to use will vary with the project and those arriving at the figures. The minimum is simply to ask an estimator to conjure up a single number. However, adding a little more rigour can significantly improve accuracy without huge additional effort.

For example, ask the estimator to provide their view on the most likely, best-case and worst-case scenarios. This is called *three-point estimating*. Let's say they come back with 'it will probably take five days, but if we get lucky maybe three days and if we run into trouble perhaps 10'. These three numbers are then averaged to provide the estimate. Given equal weight the result is six days; i.e. $(5 + 3 + 10)/3$. If there's confidence in the most likely estimate it's common to give this four times the weight. So, this time the result would be 5.5 days; i.e. $(4 \times 5 + 3 + 10)/6$.

brilliant tips

When estimating . . .

- Wherever possible involve those who'll do the work. They'll bring insight to the table, and then feel ownership of the outputs.
- Remember that people don't work productively for every minute of every day - and without a holiday. Build some downtime into the numbers.
- Combine estimating techniques to arrive at figures from different directions. If results vary widely take another look.
- Encourage realism and expect the unexpected. Make an allowance for playing less than a perfect game.
- Recruit a fresh pair of eyes. Commission a sanity check from someone who has useful experience but hasn't been involved in the estimating.

Prepare the schedule

The groundwork has now been laid so that the 'when?' part of the plan can be tackled. This is an iterative process, exploring the impact that resourcing assignments have on timescales and vice versa. The objective is to arrive at an acceptable timeline that's supported by a realistic resource plan, and with the right degree of contingency built in.

Using the activity running order and dependencies already established:

- a view is taken on the resources that will be available over time;
- those resources are sensibly allocated across activities;
- a schedule is developed based upon the elapsed time that those resources will take to complete the network of activities; and
- the total utilisation of each kind of resource over time is totted up.

The first pass through the above steps will result in an uneven use of resources. At times, some will be stretched beyond their availability, whilst others are sat idle. Options are then found for smoothing out – or *levelling* – the resource profile. For example, activities might be delayed or brought forward, and resource assignments tweaked. The process of assigning resources, and recalculating timescale and resource utilisation impacts, is repeated until a credible schedule emerges. This must meet the project need whilst demonstrating there's a realistic resource plan behind it.

As well as providing a basis for managing day-to-day work, the schedule provides a tool for the *project management team* to control the project. Important milestones are identified and marked. For example, a milestone might represent the completion of an activity that is high risk, or one upon which a large number of other tasks have a dependency. Tracking progress against milestone targets then gives a good indicator of the extent to which the schedule is being kept to.

The timeline also incorporates the *Project Board's* planned formal control points and, therefore, shows when these are expected to occur. So, for example, *Managing a Stage Boundary* tasks are represented within the schedule. Realistic timescales are incorporated for all review and approval activities.

It's usual to provide a view of the project schedule in graphical form. A Gantt chart is most commonly used. This lists activities in their running order. A timescale runs from left to right across the top, and bars are added to represent the period of time that each activity runs for. Further embellishments can be added; such as resource assignments, milestone markers and lines between bars to represent dependencies.

Analyse the risks

The planning process sheds light on project risks. For example, a dependency on a critical resource in short supply may be identified, or perhaps it's been agreed that a particular pivotal estimate can't be resolved within the desired level of accuracy. So it pays to keep hazards under review through the planning process. The same is also true for a potential upside that might be exploited.

Where a threat or an opportunity is uncovered, the plan may need adjustment to provide a suitable mitigation. So risk assessment runs alongside the planning process, with iteration between the two as plans are adjusted to reflect risks and vice versa.

PRINCE2's risk management approach is described in detail later in this chapter.

Document the plan

Now that the plan has been developed, it's documented in line with the design that was agreed at the start of the exercise. This records all of the

 **example**

A simple Gantt chart

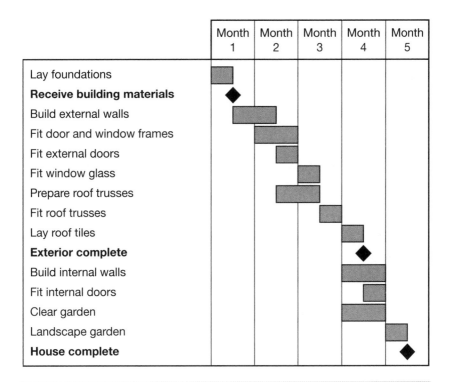

	Month 1	Month 2	Month 3	Month 4	Month 5
Lay foundations	▨				
Receive building materials	◆				
Build external walls		▨			
Fit door and window frames		▨			
Fit external doors		▨			
Fit window glass			▨		
Prepare roof trusses		▨			
Fit roof trusses			▨		
Lay roof tiles				▨	
Exterior complete				◆	
Build internal walls				▨	
Fit internal doors				▨	
Clear garden				▨	
Landscape garden					▨
House complete					◆

key aspects and also provides some explanation as to why the approach being recommended is the right one.

Experience shows that *Project Boards*, and many other stakeholders, have little interest in wading through a lengthy document and instead will be looking for a succinct summary. A presentation-style report can be used to provide an overview of the plan, the rationale behind it, and its key assumptions and risks.

The quality theme

Despite the emphasis that's often placed on deadlines and costs when a project is in flight, it won't be regarded as a triumph if it delivers *any* old thing on time and to budget. The quality of the result is the impression that sticks. This is illustrated nicely by an Australian construction project. The Sydney Opera House is widely regarded with justifiable pride as an iconic symbol of the nation, rather than a disaster that ran 10 years late and came in at more than 1,300% over budget.

PRINCE2's *Quality* theme is a direct extension of the approach taken to planning. The fundamentals are already in place through the specification of *products*; which includes setting quality expectations, defining acceptance criteria and choosing quality methods.

PRINCE2 theme

The purpose of the *Quality* theme is to define and implement the means by which the project will create and verify products that are fit for purpose.

Source: © Crown Copyright 2009. Cabinet Office.

The manual provides the following definition of what's meant by the term quality:

 Quality is generally defined as the totality of features and inherent or assigned characteristics of a product, person, process, service and/or system that bear on its ability to show that it meets expectations or satisfies stated needs, requirements or specification.

In essence, what's being talked about is a fit-for-purpose result. PRINCE2's *Quality* theme explains how delivery is achieved in line with business expectations, and in a way that allows the sought benefits to be achieved as a result. It organises its techniques under two headings:

- **Quality Planning.** Up-front preparation to agree clear quality targets, how performance will be measured, and where responsibilities lie.

- **Quality Control.** Activities executed during the project to regulate quality and to maintain supporting records.

Whilst PRINCE2 recommends that independent quality assurance is also conducted, this sits outside of the method as it's a responsibility of the wider organisation rather than of the project.

Quality planning

As with other aspects of project management, the foundations are laid at the planning stage. In fact, it's clear that PRINCE2's approaches to planning and quality are joined at the hip.

The quality discussion opens right at the beginning, as part of the *Starting up a Project* process. First, the customer's overall *quality expectations* are summarised for the project's output as a whole. They set out the big picture for what a fit-for-purpose result looks like, and are an important driver of which solution gets recommended. They include any standards that must be met, and any measures that can be used to demonstrate quality requirements have been achieved.

It may be possible to include some prioritisation of *quality expectations*. These will help when inevitable trade-offs have to be made between what's ideally wanted, and what's feasible with the time and resources that are actually available.

Next, the customer's broad quality expectations are used to develop more specific *acceptance criteria*. These are the benchmarks stakeholders will use to determine if the project has successfully delivered. Some measures provide a direct test of *product* features. Others are designed as indicators of the likelihood of achieving benefits.

Acceptance criteria are prioritised to deal with compromises that might need to be made. For example, there could be a desire for a tool to be both durable and lightweight, but one criterion may have to be traded-off to achieve the other.

 **tip**

Always define acceptance methods alongside acceptance criteria. If a criterion can't be measured objectively it doesn't belong on the list.

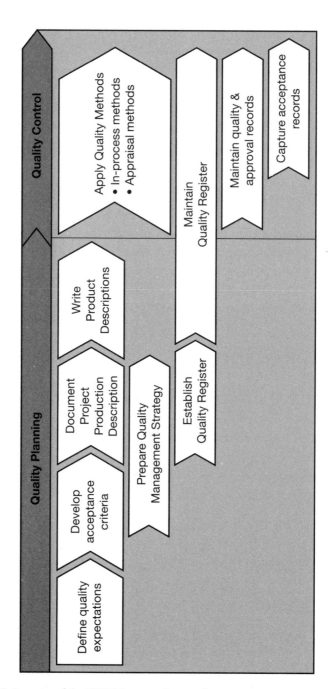

Figure 7.3 Summary of the PRINCE2 approach to quality

The customer quality expectations and acceptance criteria are then documented in the *Project Product Description*. Initial *acceptance criteria* agreed during the *Starting up a Project* process are refined during *Initiating a Project*. By the conclusion of initiation the *Project Product Description* is baselined and subject to formal change control. From a quality perspective, this is a key record. It represents the agreement of what it takes to win sign-off at closure and the methods to be used to arrive at the decision.

The final step in the quality planning process is taken when individual *Product Descriptions* are written. This is the point at which summary level *quality expectations* and *acceptance criteria* are translated into specific targets for individual deliverables. *Quality criteria* are set for each *product*. They specify the tests that will be applied to determine if *quality expectations* have been met. *Quality methods* explain how the checks will be performed. Tolerances can also be assigned to set the pass/fail boundaries.

brilliant tip

Define *quality criteria* in the form of specific questions that can be answered with a simple *yes* or *no*. This provides clarity and immediately prompts the question as to how the criteria will be measured objectively. For example, compare 'easy to understand' with 'can the document be readily understood by a customer with only basic knowledge of the subject matter?'

A *Product Description* also explains where quality responsibilities lie. These are expressed in terms of:

- **Producer:** who is responsible for the construction of the *product*.
- **Reviewer(s):** who is responsible for providing an independent assessment of whether or not the *product* has met the specification.
- **Approver(s):** who is responsible for signing-off the *product* as complete and fit for purpose.

During project initiation, a *Quality Management Strategy* is prepared. Taken alongside the project approach, this sums up how performance against quality expectations will be managed, and how responsibilities are allocated. This includes a decision on the level of formality to be adopted, with a pragmatic position being taken on the appropriate level of control.

The *Quality Management Strategy* cross-references any relevant procedures and standards already established within the organisation. It describes how these, and supporting tools and techniques, are to be applied.

 **example**

Quality management strategy – table of contents

A *Quality Management Strategy* explains the quality techniques and standards that are to be applied, and the responsibilities of those involved in achieving quality targets. It's first documented during *Initiation Stage* by the *Project Manager*, and would typically include the following sections:

Section	Typical contents
Background	The background to the project and a summary of quality expectations and acceptance criteria
Quality Management Procedures	With reference to existing procedures (as appropriate), a description of the procedures to be used for quality planning, quality control and quality assurance. Includes frequency and timing information, as well as any reporting cycles
Quality Records	An account of the records that the procedures will access, create and maintain; and where these are to be located
Roles and Responsibilities	A list of quality management roles with a description of their responsibilities (including any of relevance within the wider organisation). Identification of the individuals taking on each role
Tools and Techniques	A description of any particular tools or techniques that will be used to implement the quality management procedures

PRINCE2 requires a *Quality Register* to be established during project initiation. This provides a central record of planned quality activities and their actual results as work progresses. It's a valuable source of information for anyone undertaking any assurance or audit work.

Quality control

A set of controls is established through the investment that's made in understanding quality requirements and designing the means of measuring against these. They form an integral component of the management controls that are applied as each stage is run.

PRINCE2 classifies the methods that are used to perform quality checks in two ways:

- **In-process methods:** quality checks that are carried whilst a *product* is under development.

- **Appraisal methods:** quality checks that are performed once a *product* is complete.

It's good practice to carry out reviews sooner rather than later, and this advice applies both to individual deliverables and to sequences of related *products*. As the old saying goes, 'a stitch in time saves nine'. An early intervention avoids the expense and disruption that's incurred when a fault is detected late in the day. It therefore follows that it's beneficial to employ some *in-process methods*, rather than solely rely on *appraisals*.

In some instances it's feasible to check a product using objective and quantifiable measures. PRINCE2 uses the term *testing* to describe this kind of appraisal method. However, it's common to find that at least some element of subjective judgement is necessary. In these instances a *quality inspection* is carried out.

Whilst a *quality inspection* allows professional judgement to be used when evaluating a *product*, it's not a free-for-all. The assessment method has to be systematic, structured and planned in advance. It can be used both during and after the construction of a *product*. It can also be used alongside *testing*. For example, *testing* criteria might specify the maximum number of 'moderate' faults that can be tolerated. This makes use of quantifiable data. However, some *inspection* may be required to confirm the correct classification of faults; since these inevitably require an element of judgement.

PRINCE2 allows for any systematic inspection method to be used. However, it does offer a quality review technique that's particularly well suited to document-based *products* with an accompanying *Product Description*.

Summary of the PRINCE2 quality review technique

The players:

- **Chair** – responsible for conduct of the review.
- **Presenter** – introduces the *product* for review and responsible for addressing the review findings.
- **Reviewer** – reviews the *product*, raises findings, and agrees corrections.
- **Administrator** – provides administrative support and records outcomes.

Most of the roles would be taken on by project team members; with the *Project Manager* or *Team Manager* acting as Chair, and *Project Support* assisting as the Administrator.

The process:

- Set up a review meeting (Chair/Administrator).
- Circulate *product* and its *Product Description* (Presenter).
- Review the *product* and prepare review findings: question list for Chair and Presenter, and typographical corrections for Presenter (Reviewers).
- Consolidate question list and send to Presenter (Chair).
- Hold the review meeting:
  - Review major review findings and agree corrective actions (Chair).
  - Take a *product* walkthrough and agree corrective actions (Presenter).
  - Confirm what's been agreed (Administrator).
  - Facilitate agreement of the end result: complete/conditionally complete/incomplete (Chair).
- Co-ordinate the corrective actions (Presenter).
- Provide sign-off of corrective actions (Reviewers).
- Confirm review process concluded (Chair).
- Communicate outcome and store quality records (Administrator).
- If appropriate, request approval for the *product* (Presenter).

Quality activities generate records such as inspection results and logs of corrective actions. These are retained as documentary evidence to back-up entries in the *Quality Register*. They additionally provide useful data to other projects that want to draw on the practical experience gained.

Records of *product* approvals are also collected and held on file. Finally, as part of closure, acceptance records are obtained to document the approval of the project *product*.

The risk theme

PRINCE2's *Risk* theme provides a set of techniques for managing the uncertainty that comes with any project. These dovetail with the planning process, and fill in the detail for the *analyse the risks* step that runs throughout. There's also an important link to the principle of *continued business justification*. Understanding the level of risk that's being carried, and taking the right steps to keep this within acceptable boundaries, are essential prerequisites to a viable project with a valid *Business Case*.

> ### PRINCE2 theme
>
> The purpose of the *Risk* theme is to identify, assess and control uncertainty and, as a result, improve the ability of the project to succeed.
>
> *Source*: © Crown Copyright 2009. Cabinet Office.

In everyday speak, risks are associated with downsides. However, in PRINCE2 the term is used to cover both negative and positive impacts on project objectives. So this covers both **threats** and **opportunities**.

A systematic approach is called for, and risk management entails:

- **Identifying.** Casting a suitably wide net to spot potential threats and opportunities, and then accurately describing them.
- **Assessing.** Analysing the likelihood of risks and their potential impacts, and highlighting which deserve particular attention.
- **Controlling.** Deciding how to respond, setting up a plan of action, and ensuring it's followed through.

The need for effective risk management exists throughout the project lifecycle. There's certainly important analysis work to be done at the outset, to establish an initial view on risk and how this should shape the plan. However, threats and opportunities change over time and new ones will always pop up. So risk management cycles through identification, assessment and control until closure.

Like bacon and eggs, or gin and tonic, risks and issues are often seen in each other's company. However, PRINCE2 takes a different tack. Issues are tackled in the *Change* theme (see Chapter 9), as part of a more general approach for dealing with unplanned events.

A procedure for managing risks

PRINCE2's recommended risk management procedure is described in five steps.

- **Identify.** Determine what specific threats and opportunities the project faces. Accurately record these risks.
- **Assess.** Evaluate the probability, impact and timing of individual risks. Examine the overall risk profile.
- **Plan.** Develop management responses to the threats and opportunities.
- **Implement.** Turn plans into action, ensuring it's clear who needs to do what.
- **Communicate.** Let stakeholders know about threats and opportunities, and get the right people actively engaged in the process.

The first four steps form a natural sequence. However iteration within and between any of them is the norm; reflecting the need to re-visit previous analysis as new information emerges. Communication applies throughout to ensure a free flow of information between co-ordinators, contributors and wider stakeholders.

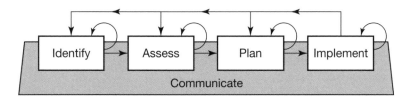

Figure 7.4 Risk management in five steps

Identifying risks

First, a well rounded picture is needed of the specific threats and opportunities that might lie in wait. Many will be apparent from the outset; especially to those who have been there previously and bought the T-shirt. However, even an experienced team wins from applying some systematic risk identification techniques. These help to ensure that nothing vital is missed. Many of these methods also provide an important side benefit: an opportunity to get the team and stakeholders involved in the project, and to build commitment to the actions designed to promote success.

 example

Risk identification techniques

Here are four straightforward techniques for identifying risks. They're widely applicable, and can be used on their own or in combination.

Lessons learned. Whilst every project is unique, the lessons learned by others can still provide a rich source of potential risks. Establish what's previously gone well and not so well – and why. An interactive discussion with those involved is the best way of getting to the heart of the matter. This exercise needs to be approached with a constructive and open mind. Beware of the 'it can't happen to me' syndrome.

Assumptions and dependencies review. In the absence of perfect knowledge, developing a plan entails making some assumptions. Not being a hard fact, an assumption poses a risk as it may turn out to be wrong. So a review of the assumptions list can highlight areas for attention. The same principle can be applied to dependencies. They carry a risk of non-delivery, or (rather less plausibly) of exceeding expectations.

Checklists. Checklists can be used as a prompt to identify individual risks and also to provide some structure for what emerges. Some are publically available, and some might be on offer within the organisation. Here's an example:

Schedule	Compatibility
Technology	Lifecycle
Organisation	Over-engineering
Resources	Users
Methods	Dependencies
	Suppliers

▶

Performance indicators. As soon as a project is underway, information becomes available about the degree of success in keeping to plan. Some financial products carry the health warning that past performance isn't a guarantee of future returns. For projects the reverse is true. Early performance is usually a pretty reliable guide to ultimate prospects – unless swift and decisive corrective action is taken where required. So for in-flight projects, indicators capable of providing an early view on performance should be placed on the risk radar.

It's critical for risks to be described in just the right way. At first, this might seem like an administrative point, but in fact the description powers the analysis that follows. It also builds the shared understanding needed. So vaguely worded or sloppily explained risks undermine all the great work that's been done to flush them out.

Whilst there'll be no prizes for literary achievement, enforcing a standard phrasing is a good means of implementing the necessary rigour. 'There is a risk that <risk cause> might result in <risk event> which would <risk impact>' is one way of approaching this. So, a woolly 'over-optimistic timescales' might get transformed into a more useful 'There is a risk that the inexperience of those estimating construction effort might result in delivery dates being unrealistic, which would cause an overrun in completing the building.'

Assessing risks

The next step is to evaluate the risks identified, both at an individual level and when taken as a whole. The objectives of the exercise are to spot the threats and opportunities that deserve particular attention, and to gain an appreciation of the overall risk profile being carried by the project.

The fundamentals of assessment involve estimating the probability of occurrence and the impact that this would have. The latter is considered across the different types of project objectives; such as cost, time, benefit and scope.

There's a wide range of analysis techniques available, ranging from the simple and intuitive to the sophisticated and complex. The best techniques to use will depend on the project, but keeping things as simple as possible is a good general principle. The risk assessment has to be understood by a variety of stakeholders, so there's a lot to be said for a method that's straightforward, even if it might lack the rigour of other more glamorous options.

brilliant tip

A very simple but effective risk assessment technique

Using professional judgement, a risk is awarded a score for its probability and impact using a simple scale:

Probability of occurrence	Impact (negative)	Impact (positive)
1: Very unlikely	−1: Negligible	1: Negligible
2: Fairly unlikely	−2: Minor	2: Minor
3: 50/50 chance	−3: Moderate	3: Moderate
4: Fairly likely	−4: Serious	4: Significant
5: Almost certain	−5: Disastrous	5: Substantial

A total risk score is than calculated by multiplying the probability score by the impact one. For example, a threat with a 50/50 chance and serious impact would be awarded a score of −12 (3 × −4), and an opportunity with very unlikely but substantial positive impact would get a score of 5 (1 × 5).

Once scores have been calculated for a set of risks, they can be sorted to reveal which threats and opportunities are top candidates for action (i.e. the ones with the largest negative and positive scores).

The probability and impact analysis can be extended to include a time dimension. It can be useful to know how soon a risk might materialise. For example, this might allow the prioritisation of actions to be refined, with precedence being given to those risks of immediate interest.

In addition to being involved in dealing with the most prominent threats and opportunities, the *project management team* has an interest in the overall risk profile. This is one part of ensuring continued business justification. Being comfortable that the project can still achieve its objectives requires the overall level of risk to sit within the bounds set by the *Project Board*. How the risk profile changes over time is also a good indicator of the general state of the project. A contained or reducing set of risks, with a good track record of tackling threats and seizing opportunities, is a sign of good health. Consistently expanding dangers with little sign of effective remedial action tells the opposite story.

Planning responses

Armed with a sound understanding of the risks faced, and an analysis of where to focus efforts, actions are planned in response. These measures aim to reduce threats and to take advantage of opportunities; whilst keeping a sensible balance between effort that's burnt and the benefits that this returns.

PRINCE2 provides a framework for countering risks, comprising nine possible types of response across threats and opportunities. They're summarised in the table below along with some simple examples:

Threat responses	Opportunity responses
Avoid. A change is made to the project so that the threat can't materialise or it no longer has an impact. *I might get run over whilst crossing the road, so I'll take the footbridge instead.*	**Exploit.** Action is taken to ensure that the opportunity arises and its impact is won. *Instead, I'll wait a few minutes and part with some loose change. That will buy me a bus journey to my destination in safety and ahead of schedule.*
Reduce. Action is taken to reduce the probability of the threat and/or its impact. *I'll spend time looking and listening really carefully before I cross the road, that way I'm pretty unlikely to get hit.*	
Fallback. A plan is prepared to reduce the impact of a threat should it occur. *Before I leave the safety of the pavement, I'll put the local hospital on standby in case it all goes wrong when I saunter out into the road.*	**Enhance.** Action is taken to improve the probability and/or its impact. *Whilst I'm waiting for the bus, I'll stick my thumb out and I might even get a lift for free.*
Transfer. A third party is lined up to take responsibility for at least some of the financial impact of the threat should it occur. *Before I leave the house, I'll make sure I've got insurance cover for my wages if I'm off work following an unfortunate accident.*	
Share. An arrangement is made to share a threat or opportunity with a third party. *A tricky one. Maybe I'll pay a friend to cross the road with me, to provide an extra pair of eyes. However, if we get hit, I'll want more than my money back!*	
Accept. A decision is made simply to live with the threat. *Having thought about it, I've decided that I should be OK crossing the road, so I will.*	**Reject.** A decision is taken not to go after the opportunity. *Having thought about it, I think I'll stick with my original plan. I'd prefer to keep my change for something more exciting.*

The above actions don't have to be used in isolation, and it may be appropriate to tackle risks with a combination. For example, a threat might be both *reduced* and anticipated with a *fallback* plan.

Having assessed the options for tackling risks, and selected the best ones, the corresponding actions are incorporated within the plan. Where a financial approach to risk management is being pursued, this might involve setting aside a risk budget to cover potential impacts and prospective responses. The funds are ring-fenced for their intended purpose, to avoid them being quickly absorbed within the overall project budget.

Any important changes in risk profile or delivery plans are reflected in an update to the **Business Case.**

Implementing the response

To assist the **Project Manager** with getting a risk response implemented, each risk is assigned a **risk owner.** This person takes responsibility for maintaining the project's understanding of the risk and for ensuring that the selected responses are carried out. The person nominated for this role should be well placed to take it on; for example, by virtue of where they sit within the organisation. However, it wouldn't be productive to over-burden one individual.

A **risk owner** can be supported by a **risk actionee,** who is assigned to carry out one or more of the response actions under the direction of the owner.

Risk communications

For the risk management process to be successful, effective two-way communication is required throughout. Intelligent input is needed from the team and stakeholders to identify the important risks, to formulate the right responses, and to ensure planned actions are executed. In return, the participants want access to the wider perspective on threats and opportunities, and to see that their input is making a difference. The **project management team** needs to foster an open and honest environment in which those at all levels feel comfortable in contributing.

Progress monitoring procedures generate official risk reports. However, information sharing extends beyond this formal route designed with project controls in mind. The **Communication Management Strategy** provides tactics for arriving at the best methods for collecting and disseminating risk-related news.

 **tip**

Keep risks on the agenda by holding regular review meetings that involve the right stakeholders. Persist with these even when the pressure is on, or it will look like risk management is an optional extra – rather than a key tool for successful project delivery.

Risk management strategy

PRINCE2 equips a project with this generic framework for managing risks. During project initiation the exact risk techniques to be used, and standards to be followed, are documented in a *Risk Management Strategy*. This is developed using any policies and procedures already established within the organisation as a starting point.

The *Strategy* includes a description of the *Project Board's* position on risk taking. This is represented as a set of risk tolerances, which set out the boundaries for what constitutes an acceptable level of risk. These find their way into plans, and will then be used to trigger escalation up the management line if risk grows beyond set limits.

 **example**

Risk management strategy – table of contents

A *Risk Management Strategy* explains the techniques and standards that are to be applied to threats and opportunities, and the responsibilities of those involved in managing risks. It's first documented during *Initiation Stage* by the *Project Manager*, and would typically include the following sections:

Section	Typical contents
Background	The background to the project and a summary of established risk management practices within the organisation
Risk Management Procedures	With reference to existing procedures (as appropriate), a description of the procedures to be used for identifying, assessing and controlling risks. Includes frequency and timing information, as well as any reporting cycles
Risk Tolerance	An overview of the *Project Board's* position on risk taking, with a definition of the risk tolerances set for the project

Tools and Techniques	A description of the techniques and any tools that will be used to implement risk management procedures; including: ● methods that will be used to assess and categorise probabilities, impacts and timing considerations ● categories to be used for risks and responses ● inventory of any performance indicators useful for identifying risks early
Risk Budget	If a risk budget is to be allocated, the funds available with an indication of how the figures have been arrived at. A description of the controls to be implemented to ensure its correct use
Risk Records	An account of the records that the procedures will access, create and maintain; and where these are to be located
Roles and Responsibilities	A list of risk management roles with a description of their responsibilities (including any of relevance within the wider organisation). Identification of the individuals taking on each role

PRINCE2 recommends the use of a *Risk Register* to hold up-to-date information relating to all of the identified threats and opportunities. It's the first port of call for the latest position on risks, and how they're being addressed.

 **impact**

Register entries

A *Risk Register* can be set up as a table, with a row for each risk. A simple spreadsheet is normally up to the job. For each threat or opportunity, you'd expect to find at least the following information:

● **ID**. A unique identifier that can be used as a reliable cross-reference.

● **Raised By**. The person who raised the risk.

● **Date Raised**. The date on which the risk was logged.

● **Description**. A clear description of the risk; ideally incorporating the cause, risk event and its impact.

● **Probability**. A probability score, representing the likelihood of the risk occurring.

● **Impact**. An impact score (or value), representing the impact on project objectives.

● **Score**. A score calculated to represent the combination of probability and impact.

- **Response**. The action(s) agreed to deal with the risk.
- **Owner**. The person assigned overall management responsibility for the risk and its treatment.
- **Open/Closed**. Whether or not the risk is current.

Additional information can be added as needed. However, avoid turning comprehensiveness into clutter. A little simplification can make the log easier to digest and to maintain – which can only be a positive result!

Summary

The *Plans*, *Quality* and *Risk* themes map out the preparatory work a PRINCE2 project invests in before it takes action. Collectively, their first significant contribution is made during construction of the *Business Case*. Exactly what has to be delivered is worked out, and the basis on which the customer would accept the results is agreed. This then enables the costs, timescales and risks involved to be assessed.

PRINCE2's *product* focus lies at the heart of its approach to building plans and managing quality. An analysis of deliverables is always the starting point, and *Product Descriptions* record what's to be constructed. They're also the place where general quality aspirations get turned into the specific measures against which a fit-for-purpose delivery will be judged.

Once a project is underway these planning techniques continue to be deployed. In turn, each *management stage* is designed down to *Work Package* level. Plans reflect the *Quality Management Strategy* and incorporate responses to the latest position on threats and opportunities.

Whilst it's vital to have a sound plan of attack, the ultimate objective is to provide control. This is delivered through baselined plans, quality methods that test against *quality criteria*, and procedures that keep risks under surveillance. This is a topic that's picked up again in Chapter 9, which explains the role that progress reporting plays in maintaining control.

brilliant recap

- There are five types of plan: *Project, Stage, Exception, Team* and *Benefits Review*.

- PRINCE2's planning cycle consists of seven steps: (1) design the plan; (2) analyse products; (3) analyse activities; (4) analyse risks; (5) prepare estimates; (6) prepare a schedule; (7) document the plan.

- *Quality Planning* starts with *quality expectations* and *acceptance criteria*, and ends with *product*-specific *quality criteria* and *quality methods*.

- *Quality Control* is applied when the wheels are in motion (*in-process methods*) and when work is complete (*appraisal methods*) – and against objective measures (*testing*) or with a degree of professional judgement (*quality inspection*).

- PRINCE2's risk management procedure takes five steps: (1) identify; (2) assess; (3) plan; (4) implement; (5) communicate.

CHAPTER 8

Subsequent delivery stage(s)

Wagons roll!

PRINCE2 topics covered in this chapter:

- *Controlling a Stage* process
- *Managing Product Delivery* process
- *Directing a Project – Give ad hoc direction* activity

About the only thing that comes to us without effort is old age.

Gloria Pitzer

Introduction

It's the moment that everybody's been waiting for. The detailed *Business Case* has been written up, the planning groundwork laid and authorisation won to run the project. Delivery can now start.

It's not a time to sit back and relax, though. However good the preparations have been, if the next phase of work isn't tightly controlled the up-front investment will soon be lost. A concerted and determined effort is required since projects aren't in the habit of delivering themselves. In fact, they show a definite preference for veering off course when left unsupervised.

With the authority delegated by the *Project Board*, the *Project Manager* is responsible for running the construction effort. Taking one *management stage* at a time, work is distributed to the team. An effective and efficient operation requires a controlled flow of work, a clear set of responsibilities, and timely intervention at the first sign of trouble.

PRINCE2's approach to achieving this is based on *Work Packages*. As the name implies, these break outputs into self-contained parcels that can be tackled by smaller teams (or by individuals). Under the control of the *Project Manager*, each *Work Package* is allocated to a *Team Manager* for delivery – or to an individual where the *Project Manager* has direct responsibility.

Progress is tracked at both *Work Package* level and for the stage as a whole. Where needed, interventions are made to keep the assignment on course, with the *Project Board* being engaged when stage or project tolerances are threatened.

PRINCE2 provides two interlocking processes to control *Work Package* delivery:

- *Controlling a Stage*; and
- *Managing Product Delivery*.

In broad terms, the former is the *Project Manager's* part in the process and the latter is designed for the *Team Manager*.

The *Directing a Project* continues to run, and this includes an activity to deal with the *Project Board* interventions that are required: *give ad hoc direction*. As each new delivery stage approaches the *Managing a Stage Boundary* process introduced at *Initiation Stage* is re-used.

This chapter describes the newcomers: the *Controlling a Stage* and *Managing Product Delivery* processes, and the *Project Board's give ad hoc direction* activity.

Controlling a stage

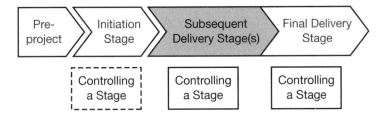

The *Project Manager* uses the *Controlling a Stage* process to oversee *product* delivery. The process covers the assignment of work, progress tracking and reporting, and tackling deviations from the plan. It's run for each delivery stage. If the *Initiation Stage* is a significant piece of work in its own right, then *Controlling a Stage* is applied there too.

Objectives for controlling a stage

- Maintaining focus on delivery of the stage's agreed *products*, and within the agreed tolerances.
- Ensuring what's delivered is fit for purpose.
- Managing risks and issues.
- Keeping *Business Case* review on the agenda.

There are eight activities:

- *Authorise a Work Package*
- *Review Work Package Status*
- *Receive Completed Work Packages*
- *Review the Stage Status*
- *Capture and Examine Issues and Risks*
- *Take Corrective Action*
- *Escalate Issues and Risks*
- *Report Highlights*

The first three (authorise, review, receive) manage the delivery cycle for each *Work Package*. The *review the stage status* activity monitors progress across *Work Packages*. It's also used ad hoc to provide a wider project perspective when advice is being sought from the *Project Board*, or a response is needed to a new issue or risk that's been captured.

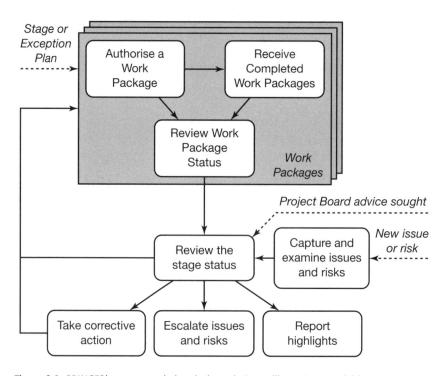

Figure 8.1 PRINCE2's recommended path through Controlling a Stage activities

Progress reviews prompt the next set of activities. Further *Work Packages* are authorised, and action is taken to correct deviations from the plan. Where a threat can't be resolved within the *Project Manager's* limit of authority, it's escalated to the *Project Board*. Finally, the *report highlights* activity publishes a regular synopsis of the project's position.

Authorise a Work Package

The *Project Manager* designs a stage as a set of *Work Packages* that need to be delivered. A golden rule is that a *product* can't be split across *Work Packages*. Therefore a larger *product* may have to be broken down into its component parts, so that a job can be neatly packaged up. In addition to the *Work Packages* that are planned at the outset, the *Project Manager* defines additional ones to deal with risks or issues that emerge as the stage unfolds.

The current *Stage Plan* or *Exception Plan* is the starting point for identifying the necessary *Work Packages*. This specifies the *products* to be delivered, and provides estimates of the resources required. Further useful information is available in the *Project Initiation Documentation* set; for example, this describes the mechanisms to be used for assuring quality and achieving *product* approval.

 example

Work Package description

The contents of a *Work Package* description will vary with the nature of the task. However, it would typically include the following information:

Information	Typical contents
Identifier	A unique code to identify the *Work Package*, with supporting version control information (e.g. date and version number)
Team Manager or Individual	Name of the person taking responsibility for completing the *Work Package*
Work Description	A summary of the work to be completed, together with *Product Descriptions* for the *products* to be delivered. May include cross-references to relevant sections of the *Stage Plan* or *Exception Plan*

Information	Typical contents
Timing and Resources	The timescales allocated for the work, including any important milestones. The resources that will be used
Tolerances	Agreed tolerances; including those for timing and resources
Approval	An account of how the **Work Package's products** will be approved and who will be responsible for this
Dependencies and Interfaces	A list of the dependencies for this **Work Package**. A description of relationships with other **products** that will be important during construction or when the outputs are used
Constraints	A list of any constraints on how the work is carried out or the people involved
Approach	A description of the techniques and tools to be used, identifying any standards that need to be adhered to. An explanation of how configuration management will be undertaken
Reporting and Controls	An explanation of how progress will be reported, and the procedures for dealing with risks and issues

The **Work Package** description is prepared by the **Project Manager**.

Whilst it's the **Project Manager's** job to define a **Work Package**, it's essential that this is done with the active engagement of the person executing it. This avoids misunderstandings and builds commitment to achieving a quality result within the parameters that have been set.

Having had the chance to digest a reasonable draft of a **Work Package** description, the **Team Manager** then prepares a **Team Plan**. This is reviewed with the **Project Manager**. Once it's complete, and the time is right, the **Project Manager** gives the authorisation to commence delivery.

The current **Stage Plan** is refined to keep it aligned with what's been agreed. The project's supporting registers may also need updating; for example, the records used to track the status of individual work items.

Review Work Package status

Once a **Work Package** is underway, progress is tracked. Following the reporting procedure that was agreed for the **Work Package**, the **Team Manager** produces regular **Checkpoint Reports**. These provide the base information for a view on how well the plan is being adhered to. In particular, a judgement is made on whether or not the *Work Package* will be delivered within the agreed tolerances. This enables the *Project Manager* to keep the current *Stage Plan* up to date and to assist in tackling any risks or issues that might emerge.

To arrive at a reliable assessment of the prospects for hitting time and resource targets, evidence is needed that quality controls are achieving their objectives. If *product* quality isn't being maintained apparent progress will be deceptive, since it won't account for the re-work that will inevitably crop up. So looking for concrete evidence of appropriate review and approval steps is an essential insurance policy.

brilliant disaster

Five warning signs that targets are going to be missed

1 Slack in the plan evaporates as soon as work starts.

2 A claim that early poor performance is just a blip that will sort itself out.

3 Evidence of corner cutting – like avoiding being slowed down by customer input.

4 Repeated broken promises.

5 Holidays being booked to coincide with critical delivery milestones.

At each review point, the *Project Manager* refreshes the *Stage Plan* with actual progress and incorporates revised forecasts. It's also treated as a useful prompt to ensure the project logs are up to date.

Receive completed Work Packages

A *Work Package* is complete when – and only when – all of its *products* have been delivered, quality assured and approved. So when a *Team Manager* says 'I'm done', it's essential that the *Project Manager* is able to:

- establish that all of the *products* exist;
- locate an audit trail that demonstrates agreed quality assurance procedures have been followed – and with a favourable result; and
- find a record of the necessary approvals.

Once the *Project Manager* is satisfied that the *Work Package* really is finished, this is recorded within the *Stage Plan* and supporting logs.

One of the rules of the game is that once a *Work Package* is signed-off, its *products* are placed under formal change control. Any requests to re-open work have to be properly evaluated and formally agreed before incurring the extra effort. This helps the *project management team* to maintain control over project scope. It creates a barrier to sneaking in last minute changes and add-ons without proper consideration of the impact. It's also an extra incentive for those approving *products* to ensure that they're definitely happy before signing on the dotted line.

brilliant tip

Advertise in bright lights the controls that swing into action once final review and approval is given. This focuses everyone's mind on getting it right first time, and reduces the risk of expensive problems lurking undetected beneath the surface.

Capture and examine issues and risks

Taking some risks and having to resolve problems that crop up are part and parcel of project life. So an important ingredient of controlling a stage is having effective procedures in place to deal with the expected unexpected. This is where the techniques in PRINCE2's *Risk* and *Change* themes are put to good use, and these are covered in depth in Chapters 7 and 9 respectively.

During a stage, issues and risks are identified by all sorts of people. They'll come from the *project management team* and those involved hands-on in *Work Packages.* Concerns may also be collected from those sitting outside of the project, such as representatives of corporate management or the target end customers.

Once an issue or risk is logged, it's assessed and reported according to the control procedures that have been agreed. This includes evaluating its severity, and the potential impact on the *Stage Plan, Project Plan* and *Business Case.* The *Project Manager* creates an *Issue Report* for an issue that's put through the formal resolution process.

The response might be to seek advice from the *Project Board*, take a *corrective action*, or to go up the escalation path. Before the right response is settled on the overall status of the stage is revisited. This enables a decision to be made in the context of the wider project.

Review the stage status

Taking progress up a level from individual *Work Packages*, headway is also tracked at stage level. This maintains an accurate picture of the overall current and forecast position against the plan – important intelligence if the *project management team* is to make informed decisions.

The status of the stage is reviewed at regular intervals, at the frequency that was agreed within the *Stage Plan*. A check can also be commissioned on an ad hoc basis; for example, when advice is sought from the *Project Board* or when preparing a response to a new issue or risk.

A number of useful information sources are available. A *Product Status Account* provides a snapshot of progress made against each of a specified range of *products*. There are also *Checkpoint Reports*, the various control logs, and the latest version of the *Stage Plan*. The *Benefits Review Plan* is also referenced to see if any benefit evaluation activities are due.

brilliant tip

Use status reviews as a cue to check that information sources are up-to-date. A regular prompt encourages housekeeping as you go, and avoids a ballooning administrative backlog.

The appraisal may identify a number of necessary follow-up actions. These might include initiating new *Work Packages*, prompting the *Project Manager* to take action to deal with a deviation from plan, or triggering escalation where tolerances are under threat.

As a stage approaches its end the review prompts the *Managing a Stage Boundary* process. Similarly, at project end the *Closing a Project* process is triggered.

Take corrective action

It's rare to find a venture that simply runs from start to finish along the path set out in its initial plan. Like a guided missile homing in on its target, a project requires frequent course corrections if it's going to arrive at its intended destination.

With the position of the current stage under close review, the *Project Manager* is soon alerted when it goes off track. The search is then on for the best tactics to bring work back into line, and within the limits of the authority delegated by the *Project Board*.

Once the most appropriate *corrective action* has been selected, the *Project Manager* arranges for this to be executed. This is typically achieved by agreeing a *Work Package* with the relevant *Team Manager*, and then authorising the work.

Escalate issues and risks

Not all issues and risks can be dealt with within the *Project Manager's* limit of authority. Where the tolerances of the stage or project are threatened, the *Project Board* is formally involved in the process of arriving at a resolution. The *Board* is alerted to an escalated issue or risk via an *Exception Report*. There may be some effort required to prepare this, so it's generally good practice for the *Project Manager* to warn the *Project Board* that an exception is heading its way.

Using the information presented in the *Exception Report*, the *Project Board* decides on the course of action to be taken. This might include:

- approving or rejecting a request to make a change to the project;
- increasing the tolerances that are under threat;
- requesting further information or analysis before a final decision is made;
- asking for an *Exception Plan* to be prepared to implement a selected option.

In a worst-case scenario, the *Project Board* may even request that the project is prematurely closed.

 **example**

Exception report - table of contents

An *Exception Report* describes the situation that threatens stage or project tolerances, and offers options and recommendations for resolving this. It's prepared by the *Project Manager* and would typically include the following sections:

Section	Typical contents
Background	A brief summary of the events leading up to the exception
Exception Description	A description of the deviation from the current plan, highlighting the tolerances that are threatened
Options Analysis	Identification of the options available. For each option: its resource, timing and benefits implications; with other key advantages and drawbacks. Includes the 'do nothing' option to illustrate the outcome if no action is taken
Recommendations	The recommended course of action with the rationale for its selection
Lessons	Lessons learned in connection with the exception and the evaluation of mitigating options

Report highlights

On a regular basis, and at a frequency agreed with the *Project Board*, the *Project Manager* issues a *Highlight Report*. This gives a picture of the position of the project and current stage, and also provides visibility of the actions that are being taken to keep within tolerances.

Much of the required data are generated by the stage status review and *corrective action* activities. This information is compiled into a form that's suitable for circulation to the *Project Board* and other stakeholders specified within the *Communication Management Strategy*.

Managing product delivery

The *Managing Product Delivery* process enables a *Team Manager* to co-ordinate *Work Package* delivery. It also controls the interface between *Project Manager* and *Team Manager*, ensuring that hand-offs between the two are handled systematically. As with *Controlling a Stage*, the process is run for each delivery stage, with the option of applying it to the *Initiation Stage* if that's a sizeable undertaking.

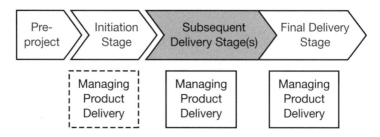

Objectives for managing product delivery

- Providing a formal procedure for allocating work packages to *Team Managers*, and for then accepting the results.
- Ensuring that what needs to be delivered is well understood, and the budgets and tolerances for the work are agreed up-front.
- Supplying accurate progress information, with appropriate escalation of any threats to a successful outcome.
- Promoting a fit-for-purpose delivery.

The process comprises three activities:

- *Accept a Work Package*
- *Execute a Work Package*
- *Deliver a Work Package*.

These are complementary to *Controlling a Stage's* three *Work Package* activities. Once authorisation to deliver is received from the *Project Manager*, the *Team Manager* negotiates final terms with the backing of a plan. *Product* development is then managed and progress reported on. Once the *Team Manager* is able to demonstrate that construction is complete, the *Work Package* is delivered back to the *Project Manager*.

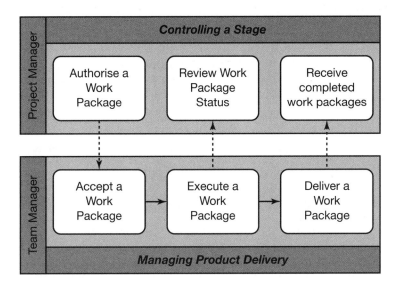

Figure 8.2 Managing Product Delivery activities and their relationship to the Controlling a Stage process

Accept a Work Package

For a given *Work Package*, the nominated *Team Manager* takes responsibility for successfully delivering its *products*. Before work can start, an agreement needs to be reached between the *Project Manager* and *Team Manager* with respect to the tolerances for the work and the constraints within which the *products* are to be delivered. The outcome is recorded in the finalised *Work Package* description.

For the *Team Manager's* protection, it's critical that a delivery commitment is given only once there is a solid plan upon which to generate estimates for timescales and resources. This in turn requires a good understanding of the *products* to be delivered, and the constraints to be worked within.

The *Project Initiation Documentation* set (including the current *Stage Plan*) and *Work Package* description are a good starting point for establishing what needs to be achieved. This is reviewed with the *Project Manager* and key stakeholders to confirm a shared understanding of the required outputs. There's also discussion of any particular requirements for how the work must be undertaken, or constraints that must be worked within.

The *Team Manager* is then responsible for developing a *Team Plan* that describes how the *Work Package* will be delivered. The format of the *Team Plan* can be replicated from that used in the *Stage Plan*. However, attaching a schedule to the *Work Package* description may well be sufficient. This might include timelines (e.g. in Gantt chart form), *product breakdown structure* and a table of resources.

The usual principles of good planning practice are followed, ensuring the involvement of team members. The assurance function may be engaged to validate the plan before it's published. It's also reviewed with the *Project Manager* to confirm its validity, and to consider if new risks have been identified or existing ones modified.

During preparation of the *Team Plan*, there's usually a degree of negotiation over the budgets for the work. A balance needs to be struck between what suits the *Project Manager* in the context of the overall plan and giving the *Team Manager* some room for manoeuvre.

brilliant tip

When a deal is being struck between *Project Manager* and *Team Manager* be on the lookout for excessive padding or the use of optimistic assumptions to force-fit an unrealistic top-down schedule. Both conspire against a productive but credible plan.

Execute a Work Package

Next, having received authorisation from the *Project Manager*, the *Team Manager* takes responsibility for executing the approved *Work Package*. Using the plan that was prepared earlier, this involves:

- overseeing the development of *products* using the agreed approach, tools and techniques;
- ensuring that *products* are put through quality management procedures and that they meet their specified *quality criteria*;
- maintaining supporting logs and registers;
- facilitating co-ordination with other related *Work Packages*;
- obtaining approvals for completed *products*.

The *Team Manager* monitors emerging risks and issues, and is free to take *corrective actions*; provided these don't threaten the tolerances agreed for the *Work Package*. If it appears that the latter are in jeopardy, the *Team Manager* escalates the issue to the *Project Manager* for a decision on what measures should be taken.

The *Team Manager* is responsible for recording progress and feeding this back to the *Project Manager*. The formal channel for this is a *Checkpoint Report*. These are produced regularly at a frequency defined in the *Work Package* description.

Deliver a Work Package

Once all of the *Work Package's products* are complete and approved, the *Project Manager* is notified. The *Team Manager* confirms that the audit trail exists to back up the claim, and so allows the *Project Manager* to receive the *Work Package*.

Directing a project – the show goes on

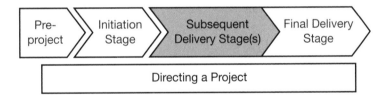

Having authorised a project, a *Project Board* remains actively engaged in steering it through its delivery stages. For example, the *Authorise a Stage or Exception Plan* activity that's employed in the *Initiation Stage* (see Chapter 6) continues to be used as each new delivery stage approaches, or in response to a revised plan that's been commissioned.

In addition to acting at preset decision points such as stage boundaries, the *Project Board* gives leadership in response to important events as they happen. PRINCE2 addresses this via an activity within the *Directing a Project* process: *give ad hoc direction*. It's called upon during delivery stages, but can be used as soon as the *Project Board* and *Project Manager* are in place. For example, there's likely to be frequent consultation during initiation when the detailed *Business Case* and plans are being developed.

Give ad hoc direction

There is a range of circumstances in which the *Project Board* is called upon to provide ad hoc direction. Some are prompted by the *Project Manager* and others originate from the *Board* members themselves. Examples of triggers include those:

- in response to a request from the *Project Manager* for informal advice;
- on receipt of an escalated *Issue Report* or *Exception Report*;
- during review of progress information within a *Highlight Report* (e.g. when a threat to the *Business Case* is identified);
- on obtaining information or instruction from corporate or programme management.

Depending on the situation, guidance may be given by the *Project Board* collectively or by individual members. Where there's benefit, additional assistance is also enlisted. For example, on receiving an *Exception Report*, *Project Assurance* might be commissioned to take a closer look at the problem and to provide an independent view on the underlying root causes. Effective decision making also requires consultation with key stakeholders, to ensure that the *Project Board* is in receipt of all of the relevant facts.

Some requests for advice can be dealt with on an informal basis – at least in the first instance. Practical guidance or assistance is given directly to the *Project Manager*. On occasions this necessitates a more detailed investigation, with the *Project Manager* then formalising the approach to the *Project Board* with an *Issue* or *Exception Report*. The *Project Board* has particular responsibility for monitoring events outside of the project, and for ensuring that the *project management team* is kept informed of relevant developments. This too may identify an issue or exception, or a need to seek further advice from up the management line.

PRINCE2 sets out in detail how issues and exceptions are handled in its *Change* and *Progress* themes, and these techniques are covered in the next chapter. Where a formal intervention is required, the *Project Board* uses these escalation and control mechanisms to steer the right course. In extreme circumstances, this might result in a decision to force a premature close to the project – either with a view to re-start or a complete stop.

Summary

PRINCE2's deliverable-based delivery approach is realised through the definition, authorisation and control of *Work Packages*. These break a *management stage* into groups of *products* that are parcelled up and distributed across the team.

The *Controlling a Stage* process is used by the *Project Manager* to design *Work Packages*, and then to take charge of their initiation. It also provides the mechanisms to monitor progress and to deal with issues and risks as soon as they emerge. This includes maintaining two-way communication between *Project Manager* and *Project Board*, and providing the escalation steps when tolerances are under threat.

PRINCE2 process-in-a-box – controlling a stage

Purpose summary: to assign work to the team, monitoring progress and intervening where necessary to ensure the stage remains within tolerance

Triggers:

Stage authorised or *Exception Plan* approved by *Project Board*

Project Board intervention requires a status review

New issue or risk arises

Preset progress review point reached or needed to support a *Project Board* decision

Activities	Key management products
• *Authorise a Work Package*	• *Work Package* descriptions
• *Review Work Package Status*	• Registers populated with issues and risks
• *Receive Completed Work Packages*	
• *Review the Stage Status*	• *Issue Reports* (as required)
• *Capture and Examine Issues and Risks*	• *Exception Reports* (as required)
	• *Product Status Account*
• *Take Corrective Action*	• *Stage Plan* and supporting records updated with progress and revised forecasts
• *Escalate Issues and Risks*	
• *Report Highlights*	• *Highlight Reports*

End results:

Work Packages authorised, executed and signed-off

Corrective actions executed

Advice or intervention sought from *Project Board* (as required)

Identification of need to start planning next stage or project closure (as appropriate)

The *Managing Product Delivery* process controls the interface between the *Project Manager* and the *Team Manager* (or individual) taking responsibility for execution of a *Work Package*. It ensures the *Team Manager's* targets are agreed before construction starts, and that the *Project Manager* is kept informed of progress with any deviations from the plan being flagged early. There's an orderly hand-over back from the *Team Manager* to *Project Manager* driven by evidence of complete and approved *products*.

PRINCE2 process-in-a-box – managing product delivery

Purpose summary: to control the interface between *Project Manager* and *Team Manager* for the initiation, execution and delivery of *Work Packages*

Trigger: *Authority to deliver a Work Package* given by the *Project Manager*

Activities	Key management products
● *Accept a Work Package* ● *Execute a Work Package* ● *Deliver a Work Package*	● *Team Plan* ● *Approved Work Package* (consistent with *Team Plan*) ● Raised issues and risks (as required) ● *Checkpoint Reports*

End result: Completed *Work Package*

The processes used during the *Initiation Stage* to direct and manage the project are deployed again. *Directing a Project* drives *Project Board* decision making, both at planned points and on an ad hoc basis. Lastly, until the *Final Delivery Stage* is reached, the project is guided through preparation for the next stage by the *Managing a Stage Boundary* process.

CHAPTER 9

Change and progress

Staying in control

PRINCE2 topics covered in this chapter:

- *Change theme*
- *Progress theme*

Change is inevitable – except from a vending machine.

Robert C. Gallagher (1939–)

Introduction

For project delivery to be controlled the *project management team* needs to know how it's doing and where it's heading. This is measured against the plan and the tolerances that have been set. It encompasses the *products* to be constructed and the benefits sought. Nevertheless, managing progress involves more than taking a ring-side seat, kicking back and enjoying the show. The intelligence gathered has to be skilfully interpreted and actively used to take charge of events.

As Chapter 7 explains, PRINCE2 supplies techniques for responding to quality issues and handling the risks that are identified. However, there's another important weapon needed in the project management armoury: a method of controlling change.

Change is a frequent visitor to projects. It presents itself in all kinds of interesting ways, and from all directions. For example, customers change their minds about what they want, and unfortunate discoveries are made about what's actually feasible once work is already underway. People move onwards, sideways and out of the door. The world around us changes too. What might have been a good bet yesterday might be viewed as a poor investment tomorrow.

This chapter first describes PRINCE2's approach to managing change. This includes a strategy for keeping a fix on the current position and a procedure for handling any kind of issue that crops up. Second, the *Progress* theme is explained. This describes how developments are assessed and reported, and how these reporting mechanisms are integrated with the controls that span change, risks and issues.

The change theme

A project has to deal with change in a systematic and considered manner. To maintain control, alterations should only be made with appropriate authority and with an understanding of the consequences. The good news is that PRINCE2's *Change* theme comes equipped with a set of tools designed for this very purpose. They include procedures for:

- **Issue and change control** – to govern how decisions about potential changes are made.

- **Configuration management** – to maintain clarity about the current position, so that accurate before and after comparisons can be made.

PRINCE2 theme

The purpose of the *Change* theme is to identify, assess and control any potential and approved changes to the baseline.

Source: © Crown Copyright 2009. Cabinet Office.

Interestingly, PRINCE2 provides a single process for handling both issues and changes. It defines an issue as an unplanned event which requires management action. This sweeps up requests for change, situations where *products* are wide of the mark or missing, and escalated problems and concerns.

Ultimate authority for responding to issues lies with the *Project Board*. It may elect to establish a *Change Authority* to handle the work when a significant volume of change is anticipated. The *Change Authority*, a suitably qualified person or team, is delegated at least some of the *Board's* decision making powers.

It's generally good practice to set up a *change budget*. This is funding that's pre-agreed between customer and supplier to cover changes and the analysis work en route. It's a realistic up-front statement that everything can't be nailed down on the first day, and gives a degree of flexibility for all concerned. Of course, prudent controls are needed to ensure this contingency is used wisely and for its intended purpose.

brilliant tip

When recruiting personnel and planning how responsibilities will be distributed, anticipate what issue management might involve. Your most skilled and knowledgeable people will have an important contribution to make. So issue resolution will grind to a halt if these resources are stretched from day one.

A procedure for managing issues

PRINCE2 defines three types of issues:

- **Request for change:** a proposal to make an alteration to the current baseline.

- **Off specification:** a situation where a *product* is (or will be) missing or failing to meet its specification.

- **Problem/concern:** anything else that the *Project Manager* needs to resolve or escalate.

A common procedure is provided for resolving these, and it consists of the following five steps:

- **Capture.** Take a quick look and form an initial view on severity and priority.

- **Examine.** Take a closer look, consider the impacts, and re-visit severity and priority.

- **Propose.** Evaluate the options available, and recommend a course of action.

- **Decide.** Agree what will be done (or make a conscious decision to stick with the status quo).

- **Implement.** Pursue the agreed course of action.

Depending on the level of formality being adopted, issues are tracked using either an *Issues Register* or the *Project Manager's Daily Log*.

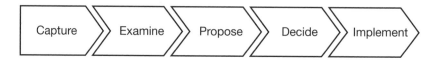

Figure 9.1 The steps of PRINCE2's issue resolution procedure

Capture an issue

Many issues can be handled directly by the *Project Manager,* and without use of a weighty formal procedure. This provides a quick and efficient response. PRINCE2 incorporates this common sense approach, with the added benefit that the *Project Board's* powder can be kept dry for those occasions when more significant matters arise.

So the first step is to take an initial view on the severity of the issue. If it's something straightforward, the *Project Manager* records the problem or concern in the *Daily Log*, and goes about getting a resolution. Where it's determined that the formal route is required, the issue is entered within the *Issues Register*.

An *Issue Report* is then created. This will be used to capture analysis work and resulting decisions. At this stage it's populated with what's currently known. This task might fall to the person who raised the issue, and who therefore has valuable first-hand knowledge.

 example

Contents of an issue report

An *Issue Report* holds what's known about an issue. It's used when a request for change, off-specification or problem/concern is being handled formally. Here's the kind of information you'd expect to find:

- **ID**. A unique identifier as specified in the *Issue Register's* corresponding entry.
- **Issue Type**. Request for change, off-specification or problem/concern.
- **Raised By**. The person who raised the issue.
- **Date Raised**. The date on which the issue was logged.
- **Description**. A clear description of the issue, ideally incorporating its cause.
- **Priority**. A priority rating, e.g. Must/Should/Could/Won't tackle.
- **Severity**. A severity rating, e.g. Negligible/Minor/Moderate/Serious/Disastrous.
- **Impact Analysis**. An assessment of the impact of the issue on the project, with discussion of any wider implications (e.g. on other projects).
- **Recommendations**. The advised action(s) to deal with the issue, with supporting rationale.
- **Decision**. A description of the agreed response to the issue, with date of decision and approval body.
- **Open/Closed**. Whether issue is current or closed (with date on which completion was verified).

The document is created when an issue is first captured, and is updated over time to reflect the state of analysis and decision making. The report is finalised once it has been verified that the issue is closed.

Examine an issue

The next step is to work out what impact the issue has – and/or might have – on the project. A broad perspective is taken to compile an accurate picture. The implications for all stakeholders are considered; looking at the issue from business, user and supplier viewpoints. It's also possible that impacts will be felt externally, for example, in other projects or parts of the organisation. Thought is given to longer-term consequences too. For example, chopping a *product* from scope might provide an attractive quick fix, but what's the year-on-year operational impact once the customer has to live with this decision long-term?

For the immediate project concerns, the analysis is conducted using three lines of enquiry:

- What's the impact in relation to the targets that have been set for time, cost, quality and scope?
- What's the impact on the *Business Case*, including the benefits that are expected?
- What's the impact on the level of risk that the project is carrying?

The work required to arrive at definitive answers to the above may itself present an issue. For example, valuable resources may have to be diverted, or tasks put on hold, whilst an answer is awaited. The *Project Manager* has to tread the line between obtaining sufficient information to formulate a recommendation, whilst avoiding beginning issue resolution prematurely.

The result of the impact analysis allows the severity and priority of the issue to be refined, with advice being sought from the *Project Board* if required.

Propose a course of action

Next, options for dealing with the issue are developed. With input from problem and solution experts, alternative approaches are identified and evaluated. Each alternative can be thought of as having its own mini *Business Case*. Enough information is obtained to allow comparison of the trade-offs between costs, benefits and risks. The option that gives the best return is put forward as a recommendation.

 **brilliant** tip

Options analysis deserves some imagination and creativity. Harness the power of a well motivated team working collaboratively, and in an environment where no one gets shot down. It's surprising how often adversity can be turned into opportunity.

Where it looks as though the project or current stage has to enter territory that's out of tolerance, an *Exception Report* could be prepared. This travels alongside the *Issue Report,* and presents the *Project Board* with the information it needs to make its decision.

Make a decision

Minor issues can be resolved directly by the *Project Manager,* who selects the best response. However, an escalation going through the formal procedure will arrive at the door of the *Project Board* or *Change Authority.*

PRINCE2 maps out the valid responses to each type of escalated issue or exception. A *request for change* is approved or rejected, and an *off-specification* is given a concession or an instruction to resolve. It's possible that a decision is deferred (e.g. perhaps it's not the best time to commit one way or the other), or further information requested. Where a resolution lies outside of the *Change Authority's* remit an *Exception Report* is requested to kick off the next escalation process.

The submission of a problem or concern elicits the guidance sought or results in a request for an *Exception Plan.*

Implement the response

The final step is for the *Project Manager* to oversee implementation of the agreed resolution (where necessary). Plans are adjusted as appropriate. An existing *Work Package* may be revised or a new one created. Alternatively, an *Exception Plan* is prepared where this has been requested. The *Issue Register* and *Issue Report* are updated to reflect the decisions reached and ultimately the closure of the issue.

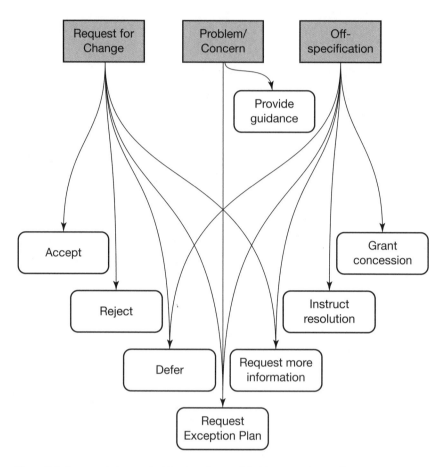

Figure 9.2 Issue and change decision tree for escalated issues and exceptions

Configuration management

A project builds many interrelated components, and each of these has its own lifecycle from initial creation through to review and approval. The configuration of the outputs has to be properly managed if the above issue and change control procedure is to be effective. This ensures there's a sound baseline against which impacts can be assessed. It also provides information on the relationships between *products*, and so gives a useful trail to follow when looking for potential knock-on effects.

brilliant disaster

Configuration management – ignore it at your peril!

Imagine your washing machine has let you down and you've taken the brave step to fix it yourself. You've obtained a maintenance manual, diagnosed the fault and ordered in the spare parts. What could possibly go wrong?

Further imagine that, once your machine is lying in bits on the kitchen floor, it dawns on you that your manual actually relates to a different model. Some of the parts supplied look way too modern for your machine, and some look suspiciously like those you'd find in a dishwasher.

Configuration management isn't the world's most exciting subject, but without it anything but the simplest project is at risk of confusion, self-inflicted re-work and quality clangers.

PRINCE2 isn't prescriptive about the configuration management procedure that should be adopted, but it does set expectations for the activities that are included:

- **Planning**. To settle on the detailed approach, including deciding what level of control is appropriate. For example, do components need to be tracked at the nut, bolt and washer level – or is it sufficient to track their group assemblies?

- **Identification**. To build an inventory of the components – the *configuration items* – at the right level. Applying a coding system so that individual items can be uniquely identified and described.

- **Control**. To ensure that finalised *products* can be changed only if formal authorisation has been granted. Providing a facility for baselining specific configurations at a given point in time, and preserving these for future reference.

- **Status accounting**. To report on the state of *products* and their history. In particular, finding out exactly where you currently stand.

- **Verification and audit**. To demonstrate that configuration records are being maintained accurately, and that planned controls are doing their intended job.

Starting with any standard approaches already implemented within the organisation, decisions on exactly how a project will go about configuration management are made during initiation. This is documented within a *Configuration Management Strategy*, which also describes other controls for issues and changes. Procedures are then reviewed at the end of each stage, with refinements being made if needed.

 brilliant example

Configuration management strategy – table of contents

A *Configuration Management Strategy* describes how *products* are controlled and secured, and who is responsible for this. It's developed during *Initiation Stage* by the *Project Manager*. The document would typically include the following sections:

Section	Typical contents
Background	The background to the project and a summary of established configuration management and change control practices within the organisation
Configuration Management Procedures	With reference to existing procedures (as appropriate), a description of the processes to be used for identifying, controlling, and reporting on *products* and their configurations. Includes frequency and timing information, as well as any reporting cycles
Issue and Change Control Procedures	With reference to existing procedures (as appropriate), a description of the processes to be used for capturing and evaluating issues/changes, making decisions on their resolution, and overseeing implementation. Includes frequency and timing information, as well as any reporting cycles
Tools and Techniques	A description of the techniques and any tools that will be used to implement the procedures, for example: • methods for scoring the priority and severity of issues • software tools for automating aspects of configuration management
Change Budget	If a change budget is to be allocated, the funds available with an indication of how the figures have been arrived at. A description of the controls to be implemented to ensure its correct use
Records	An account of the records that the procedures will access, create and maintain; and where these are to be located. Includes details of the *Issue Register* and *Configuration Item Records*
Roles and Responsibilities	A list of change management and change control roles with a description of their responsibilities (including possible *Change Authority* and any of relevance within the wider organisation). Identification of the individuals taking on each role

The progress theme

So what triggers PRINCE2's change – and other – control techniques? The link is made clear by a well known saying: 'if you can't measure it, you can't manage it'. The *Progress* theme sets out when and how the measuring is done, and explains the management actions that handle the results.

PRINCE2 theme

The purpose of the *Progress* theme is to establish mechanisms to monitor and compare actual achievements against those planned; provide a forecast for the project objectives and the project's continued viability; and control any acceptable deviations.

Source: © Crown Copyright 2009. Cabinet Office.

Some controls activate in conjunction with reports published at a pre-planned frequency; for example in response to a monthly update to the *Project Board*. Others are applied when a specific event is recorded; for example when a new issue arises or a stage completes.

PRINCE2 specifies the progress reports that are generated and the information that these contain. It also explains how its reporting regime dovetails with the controls exercised by the *project management team*.

Progress review and reporting

The *Project Manager* regularly monitors progress against that planned. The actual versus planned comparison is made against a baseline that's set at three levels:

- **Project.** The *Project Plan* specifies project level targets and tolerances.
- **Stage.** The current *Stage Plan* sets specific targets and tolerances for that stage.
- **Work Package.** *Work Package* descriptions define what each component of a stage is to deliver, and the tolerances within which this must be achieved.

PRINCE2's processes generate the source management information that's needed. *Work Package* news is delivered by the *Team Manager* via *Checkpoint Reports*. The *Project Manager* supplements this with further data from records, registers and logs.

 **brilliant** tip

Evidence of progress

Interrogation of the project records, registers and logs gives useful insight into progress. Sample questions for the prosecution (or defence) are:

- **Issue Register:** are the number and nature of open issues consistent with a project that's on track?

- **Quality Register:** does the quality failure rate inspire confidence in a delivery that's on time and fit for purpose?

- **Risk Register:** considering the overall risk profile, what's the betting that the plan is achievable?

- **Daily Log:** is there a credible track record of logging smaller actions (e.g. relating to issues being handled informally) and putting them to bed?

- **Configuration Item Records:** when a *Product Status Account* report is run, what does it reveal about where products are in their lifecycle against where they're planned to be at this point?

Like any crime scene investigation, reliance on any single clue in isolation can risk a miscarriage of justice. The right conclusion is arrived at by combining evidence, and looking for patterns and trends.

The *Project Manager* keeps the *Stage Plan* updated to reflect progress. Then, on a regular basis, a *Highlight Report* is prepared for the *Project Board*. This summarises the headway made and the outlook for the next reporting period.

The frequencies for generating *Checkpoint* and *Highlight Reports* are set so they're consistent with the level of control being sought. This is determined by the level of plan being tracked, and perhaps the personnel involved too. So whilst it would be reasonable for a *Team Manager* to report weekly, it might be considered over-kill for a *Project Board* to request *Highlight Reports* from a seasoned *Project Manager* more than monthly. Reporting frequencies don't have to be set in stone. With the agreement of the recipients, cycles can be upped or slowed according to the phase that's been reached.

 **examples**

Checkpoint Report and Highlight Report – table of contents

Checkpoint Reports and *Highlight Reports* provide information on the status of a *Work Package* and *Stage* respectively. They have a similar layout and would typically include the following sections:

	Typical contents	
Section	**Checkpoint Report**	**Highlight Report**
Date	The date on which the report was prepared	
Period Covered	The reporting period covered	
Tolerance Status	Current and forecast view of performance against each of the *Work Package's* tolerances	Current and forecast view of performance against each of the project's and stage's tolerances
Progress this Period	*Products* completed (approved) this period *Products* in progress (perhaps with percentage complete) *Products* not started as planned Any other notable achievements (e.g. recruitment of resources)	*Work Packages* completed and in progress this period *Products* completed (approved) this period *Products* not started as planned *Corrective actions* taken Any other notable achievements (e.g. recruitment of resources)
Change Requests	N/A	Change requests raised, approved/rejected and pending
Issues and Risks	Status of active issues and risks relating to the *Work Package*	Status of significant active issues and risks
Outlook for Next Period	*Products* forecast to be complete (approved) during next period *Products* forecast to be started in next period Any notable events forecast for next period	*Work Packages* forecast to be complete and initiated during next period *Products* forecast to be complete (approved) during next period *Corrective actions* to be completed during next period Any notable events forecast for next period

Highlight Reports are prepared by the *Project Manager*, and *Checkpoint Reports* are the responsibility of the *Team Manager*.

A comparison against plan is included in two other reports that are prepared at defined points in the project lifecycle. They're produced by the *Project Manager* for the *Project Board*:

- **End Stage Report.** An account of what a stage has delivered, accompanied by an overall statement of the project position.
- **End Project Report.** An assessment of what the project has delivered, and the extent to which it met its original objectives.

These reports are used to facilitate stage or project closure decisions.

Finally, there's a virtuous circle to be harnessed during progress reviews. The latter trigger consideration of what went well and not-so-well. The resulting lessons are documented in the *Lessons Log* and presented in *Lessons Reports.* These then provide a useful input when actions are planned in response to progress.

It shouldn't happen on a project (but did) . . .

A large multinational was preparing to roll-out a new accounts system across its territories. A central IT team had the job of configuring the package for each country, and then going on tour to install and to train locally. As the date for the first excursion approached, the development manager confidently reported to his *Project Manager* that his team was ready for lift-off. In fact, he was so confident he had already bought airline tickets for himself and his side-kick. Shortly afterwards, a chance conversation between the *Project Manager* and a couple of developers revealed a very different picture. It was news to the technicians that their package was ready. In fact, they hadn't even started work on it.

As important as the official record is, it doesn't tell the whole story. Engaging in a little informal contact with the team can yield fruitful intelligence. It's amazing what a friendly chat over a coffee can sometimes reveal.

Real or just apparent progress?

Can progress reports really be trusted? This is a common question asked by managers who've been stung by projects that merrily forecast an on-track delivery up to the eleventh hour – at which point a huge slippage is suddenly unveiled. This highlights why successful progress reporting is as much about accurate predictions as a commentary on past performance.

In particular, it's dangerous to rely exclusively on *percentage complete* estimates. These tend to focus on the effort that's been put in rather than the remaining distance to the finishing line. This gives rise to the common phenomenon of activities that race towards 100% complete only to get stuck at the 80% mark. By this point, the person reporting progress is still frantically toiling away at an expanding task, and fears a demand to see a near-finished *product* will be made if a number close to one hundred is mentioned.

In looking for reliable indicators of progress, it's better to rely on estimates of outstanding work. Here's a simple example at *Work Package* level:

 **example**

A *Team Manager* is told that a task is going to take ten days' effort to complete and that four days will be spent on that task this week.

At the end of the week, a progress update is requested. This news is that:

- three days were spent working on the task
- there are now eight days of outstanding work remaining

The *Team Manager* now knows that:

- only three out of the planned four days were spent on the task; and
- only two days of productive work were actually achieved (since this is the amount by which the outstanding work has been reduced).

To get a grip on future prospects, the *Team Manager* needs to find out what's behind the failure to apply the planned effort, and to investigate the expanding estimate for the remaining work.

PRINCE2's principle of *focus on products* makes a great contribution to achieving rigorous and reliable reporting. A *Work Package*, stage and project are only finished once they've delivered every *product* they committed to – and that includes navigating quality assurance and achieving sign-off. So using *only* completed *products* within a progress measure provides a sound basis for understanding what's been achieved. This might generate a rather pessimistic view of accomplishments early on, when there's plenty of work in motion, but it does guard against counting chickens before they've hatched.

PRINCE2 doesn't mandate particular techniques for evaluating progress. However, it's good practice to select an approach that gives weight to *product* completion, and forecasts that use measures of outstanding rather than completed work. If progress is summarised visually that helps with communication too.

brilliant tip

Techniques for representing progress

Different techniques can be blended to build a picture of performance to date and current forecasts. Here's an example that combines:

- a milestone chart for timelines;
- a bar graph for outstanding days of effort at the end of each time period;
- a table summarising performance for the current period.

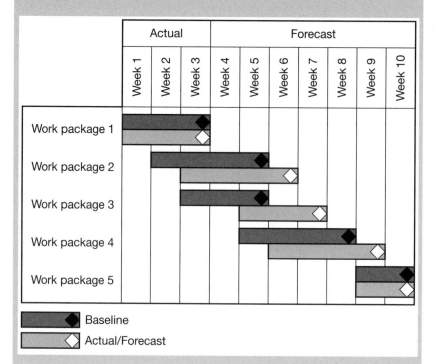

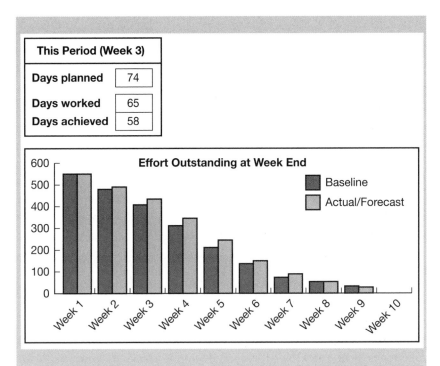

This Period (Week 3)	
Days planned	74
Days worked	65
Days achieved	58

Looking across the three measures, a picture emerges of current progress and likely outcomes.

Even though the first milestone was hit, it looks as though this project stage started to slip early on. The outstanding work isn't being eaten into quickly enough – perhaps through a combination of difficulty in securing resources, and then finding the going tougher than expected. The *Project Manager's* forecast that baselined timescales can be rescued warrants a closer look. Is the required turnaround in resourcing and work rate realistic?

Progress and control

Monitoring progress and forecasting future performance is the first step to controlling a project. However, what keeps it on track is taking the right corrective action and doing this in a timely fashion. So PRINCE2 integrates its management controls with its mechanisms for tracking progress against plan.

brilliant tip

When deciding upon the content and layout of progress reports, be guided by their ultimate purpose. They're a communication tool designed to prompt constructive action. Ensure that the key facts stand out and the audience isn't drowned in distracting (or sleep-inducing) detail.

First, the processes that describe what reports get generated when, also specify who's on the receiving end and how they should respond. So for example, the *review the stage status* activity (within the *Controlling a Stage* process) flows to others for taking corrective actions and escalating issues and risks.

Second, progress reporting is tied to PRINCE2's fundamental control method: delegation of authority. Through the agreement of tolerances, management responsibility is distributed appropriately along the chain of command. Control mechanisms then ensure that if news is received that tolerances at one level are threatened, this is escalated upwards to the next management tier for a considered response. How the deviation is handled depends on the level of plan that's impacted:

- **Work Package** (only): the *Project Manager* is responsible for agreeing a corrective action to deal with an issue raised by a *Team Manager*.

- **Stage** (but not project): the *Project Board* is responsible for agreeing the response to an *Issue Report* and *Exception Report* prepared by the *Project Manager*.

- **Project**: the issue is outside of the *Project Board's* authority, so it refers the situation up the line.

Any change to the baseline that's reported against is carefully controlled. *Project Board* approval is required for any revisions to targets and tolerances for a project or given stage. The audit trail for a change is maintained through the preparation and approval of an *Exception Plan*.

PRINCE2's principle of managing by stages delivers another important progress control. This supports the above framework of delegation and reporting; whereby the *Project Manager* oversees delivery on behalf of the *Project Board* one stage at a time. Furthermore, the boundaries between

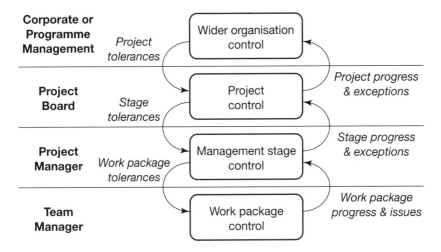

Figure 9.3 Delegation and reporting levels

stages implement major control points. The *Managing a Stage Boundary* process ensures that the *Project Board* receives the information it needs to confirm that the project remains viable and still has a valid *Business Case*. It also guarantees that any stage has a solid plan (with agreed tolerances) before it can start.

brilliant tip

Stages – how many and how long?

PRINCE2 mandates that all projects have at least two management stages: one for initiation, and another to deliver and close. However, a project is free to break its delivery work up into as many stages as it sees fit.

Numerous stages provide plenty of control points, but come with a management overhead. On the other hand, piling all eggs into a single delivery basket carries risk, since the managing by stage control is weakened. So there's a pragmatic balance to be struck between management effort and level of control. Good questions to ask when deciding on the number of stages and their length are:

- **What's the size and complexity of the challenge?** A single delivery stage might suit a small and simple project. However, the greater the challenge, the stronger the case for breaking the work up.

- **Are there some obvious, natural phases of work?** There could be benefit in aligning management stages with these; for example design, build and test.
- **What are the key decision points?** These provide good candidates for stage boundaries.
- **What's a realistic planning horizon?** A stage needs to be planned in detail, so it can't be longer than the timeframe over which this is feasible.
- **What are the big project risks?** Stages could be designed to contain these, and to allow impact on business justification to be re-visited at the right time.
- **How's the project going to be resourced?** Maybe it's beneficial for stage design to reflect the way that people or financial resources will be secured.
- **Are there any important commercial considerations?** Perhaps stages need to align to procurement cycles or to support contractual terms negotiated with suppliers.
- **What important external factors are there?** For example, it might be necessary to synchronise construction phases in line with activities on another related project.

Within a stage, the *Project Manager* exercises control at *Work Package* level. Construction can't begin until terms of reference are agreed with the *Team Manager* (or individual responsible) for what's to be delivered, and the boundaries for time and resources. *Checkpoint Reports* provide the trigger for intervention where needed, and a *Work Package* is ticked off only once there's proof that all *products* are quality assured and approved.

Summary

The *Change* theme rounds off the set of tools PRINCE2 provides to control a project. A common procedure handles change requests, deviations from specification, and all other escalated problems and concerns. The impact of an issue, and the options available, are carefully assessed before any change is permitted. The configuration of the project's outputs is properly managed, so that decisions start with an accurate assessment of the current position.

PRINCE2's progress reporting regime equips the *project management team* with the intelligence it needs to direct and manage the project, and to trigger appropriate *corrective actions*. Information paths feed the controls embedded in PRINCE2 processes, including those delivered through delegation of authority and management by stages.

Collectively, the management controls and the facts that drive them protect the investment made in the *Business Case* and plans. The base-line used to authorise the project at initiation is only changed with appropriate authority, and with the objective of ensuring the project's on-going viability.

 brilliant recap

- There are five steps to controlling issues and changes: capture, examine, propose, decide and implement.

- Change is assessed against the baseline set, and without effective configuration management a reliable answer can't be obtained.

- Issue management doesn't have to be a cumbersome and bureaucratic process – sometimes informal intervention by the *Project Manager* is both desirable and allowable.

- Progress reports are as much about looking forward as backwards – and what's left to do is more important than what's already been done.

- Progress control isn't a spectator sport – it's all about making timely and intelligent interventions to ensure a project remains viable (or to bring it to a swift close).

CHAPTER 10

Final delivery stage

A controlled stop

PRINCE2 topics covered in this chapter:

- *Closing a Project* process
- *Directing a Project* process – *authorise project closure* activity

There are two kinds of people, those who finish what they start and so on.

Robert Byrne (1930 –)

Introduction

In many ways, the *Final Delivery Stage* is just like any other – and for a simple project, it will be the *only* delivery stage. On behalf of the *Project Board*, the *Project Manager* continues to oversee the authorisation, execution and acceptance of *Work Packages*. Quality is controlled, risks are managed, issues dealt with, and progress tracked. However, there's one critical difference: a point is reached when the project is brought to a controlled finish.

A defining feature of projects is that they have *defined* start and end points. The latter is just as important as the former. Without an end marker a project would lose its management focus, drift into 'business as usual', and become part of the furniture. The pivotal control of customer acceptance would be weakened, with pressure being removed to hit delivery targets on schedule and within budget. Running an on-going operation with a project organisation is also an inefficient use of resources.

 **tip**

An early step-by-step review of customer acceptance criteria, and how these will be judged, avoids unfortunate disagreements at project end. Whilst these have been agreed from the outset, it's useful insurance to confirm that customer and supplier are still shooting for the same goal posts.

Bringing about controlled closure requires careful preparation, and the necessary tasks are included within the *Final Delivery Stage* plan. These include completing customer hand-over, checking that all planned *products* are ticked off, releasing resources and evaluating project performance. PRINCE2 has a dedicated process for these activities and it runs in place of *Managing a Stage Boundary*. It's called *Closing a Project*, and is used for both planned and premature closures.

Clearly, the decision to end a project is a vital control point for the *Project Board*. Before turning the lights out, it needs to ensure that what's been promised has been delivered and the customer has signed-off formal acceptance. It also has a responsibility to confirm the final *Business Case* position, communicate the end result, and pass on lessons that will benefit others. The *Directing a Project* process supplies an activity to handle the last decision point: *authorise project closure*.

This chapter describes the *Closing a Project* process and the final part of *Directing a Project*.

It shouldn't happen on a project (but did) . . .

In its closing stages, a venture lost its *Project Manager*. The *Executive* decided that a replacement was an unnecessary luxury. Instead, she published a project calendar to the team. She was confident that it nicely summarised the outstanding work and provided a realistic set of dates to hit.

Without anyone there to mediate, friction between customers and suppliers soon erupted. Amidst growing recriminations and finger pointing progress went into reverse. Faced with having to issue a fourth version of her project calendar, the *Executive* finally relented. A *Project Manager* was parachuted in. He wrestled back control, soothed tempers and got the work completed – albeit at greater cost than had originally been envisaged.

Even projects close to completion need careful management. In fact, the phase that achieves final customer sign-off can be the most challenging.

Closing a project

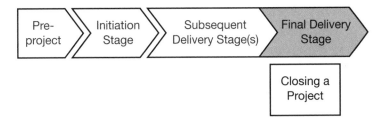

The *Closing a Project* process provides a set of activities for bringing a project to a controlled end. It's used both for closing a project once it's met its objectives, and in the scenario where an early termination has been agreed.

Objectives for closing a project

- Confirming that the project has delivered everything that's been agreed; and that arrangements have been made to deal with any open issues, risks and actions.
- Ensuring that the customer is able to use and to support the *products* handed over once the project team disbands.
- Verifying that all benefits achieved to date have been recorded, and that a plan is in place to track future ones.
- Assessing performance against the original baseline and any subsequent revisions to this.

The process checks a project's outputs are complete, assesses its performance, extracts final lessons, and tidies up loose ends. It consists of five activities:

- *Prepare planned closure*
- *Prepare premature closure*
- *Hand over products*
- *Evaluate the project*
- *Recommend project closure.*

These activities are included within the plan that's developed for the final stage of delivery. Where the project is brought to an early halt, the process is still followed. However, PRINCE2 recognises that pragmatic tailoring of the approach is required to reflect the particular circumstances.

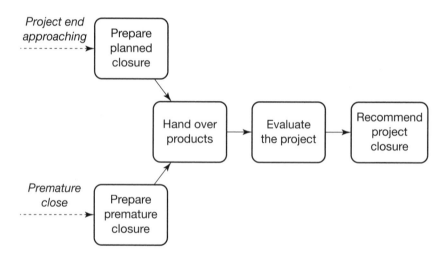

Figure 10.1 PRINCE2's recommended path through Closing a Project activities

The main resulting *products* are an *End Project Report* (including lessons) and updated *Project Plan* and *Benefits Review Plan*, together with a closure recommendation.

Prepare planned closure

Remember the *Project Product Description* that was documented way back during the *Initiation Stage?* The *Project Manager* needs to be satisfied that this has been successfully delivered against. Everything that was promised has to be provided and the agreed acceptance criteria met. To assist in making this assessment, *Project Support* runs off a *Product Status Account*. This confirms (or otherwise) that all of the planned *products* have been delivered, met their *quality criteria*, and have gained the necessary approvals.

In preparation for closure, the *Project Plan* is also updated with actual progress from the *Final Delivery Stage*.

Prepare premature closure

When the *Project Board* calls for a project to be halted, anything of value is rescued. Wider impacts of early cancellation are considered too. This requires bringing work to a graceful conclusion, rather than simply abandoning ship.

As with a planned closure, a review of an up-to-date *Product Status Account* is a pretty good place to start. This confirms what's already been constructed and what's currently in play. Tactics are agreed for each deliverable that's in progress. In some cases, it's worthwhile putting in a little additional work to put a *product* into a known state, or even to complete it. The *Project Board* is engaged in the decision so the right balance is struck between getting value out of the sunk investment and engineering a timely stop.

The *Project Manager* agrees a plan for completing the outstanding work with the *Project Board*. This includes updating the *Project Plan* with actuals, and finalising logs and registers.

It's possible that cancellation has implications that go beyond the project. For example, another initiative may be expecting to use the results. The relevant stakeholders are contacted, including those up the management line, so that they're aware of the change of plan. This includes notification of the early release of resources.

Hand over products

A project isn't complete until all the *products* destined for the customer are handed over, and in such a way that they're useable and supportable. Hand-over can take place in one 'big bang' near the end, or as a series of phased deliveries. When a project is being halted early, a hand-over approach is agreed that's consistent with the closure tactics signed off by the *Project Board*.

With all the excitement around getting *products* out of the door, it can be easy to overlook what happens once the customer receives them. This is a shame because all the hard work put in is undermined if the hand-over is mismanaged.

Here, first impressions count. If initial performance falters it's then an uphill struggle to win round the doubters. Unfortunately, there's no honeymoon period. However good testing and assurance procedures are, faults are most likely to emerge during the first use in anger.

This all underlines the importance of up-front planning for hand-over and the support organisation that's needed. PRINCE2 encourages thought about this right from the *Initiation Stage*.

 **tip**

Add successful initial operation to the acceptance criteria that are negotiated from *Pre-project*. That way, there's pressure to keep the experienced team in place until hand-over is judged to be a success.

The hand-over of *products* is backed up by records to confirm acceptance both from customer and support organisations. The transfer of ownership is recorded in the *products' Configuration Item Records*.

This activity also provides a trigger for ensuring the *Benefits Review Plan* contains the latest information on benefits delivered to date, and those expected in the future. This might incorporate information gained from seeing the outputs put to practical use.

Finally, the *project management team* identifies any actions needed after project closure. It's agreed how best to pass these on and to ensure that they're actively owned.

Evaluate the project

The last steps before recommending closure are to assess how successful the project has been, and to determine what lessons should be drawn from the experience. Achievements can be viewed from a number of perspectives. However, these boil down to two fundamental questions:

- Has/will the project's *Business Case* be achieved?
- Was the project delivered within the targets set for it?

These questions are considered in the context of the original baseline set during the *Initiation Stage*, and any subsequent revisions that were later approved as the project proceeded.

brilliant tip

Important questions to ask during project evaluation

- To what extent are the benefits originally forecast in the *Business Case* now expected to be achieved? Has the timing of delivery changed?
- Did new benefits or *dis-benefits* appear?
- Were all of the planned *products* delivered? Were there any significant quality issues encountered (e.g. instances of substantial re-work)?
- How does actual performance compare with the baselined targets and tolerances?

- How well did individuals perform as a team?
- In the case of a premature close, what train of events led to the decision to stop?
- What follow-on actions need to be assigned?

The whole *project management team* is involved in the evaluation exercise, with additional input being sought from key stakeholders.

Once the performance of the project has been reviewed, a concluding set of lessons learned are captured. Building on the assessment that's been made throughout, final consideration is given to what went well and not so well. This includes judging the effectiveness of management strategies, controls and techniques. The successes and failures, and their underlying causes are written up in a *Lessons Report*.

Finally, the results of the project evaluation are documented in an *End Project Report*, and this includes a summary of the lessons learned.

 **example**

End project report – table of contents

The *End Project Report* summarises the project's performance against its agreed baseline(s). It's prepared by the *Project Manager* during the *Final Delivery Stage*, and typically includes the following sections:

Section	Typical contents
Executive Summary	A short (one page) summary of the performance of the project against the objectives that were set for it; highlighting the top lessons learned and any important actions needed beyond project closure
Background	The reason for the project, its primary objectives and a brief narrative of project events. An account of any changes that were approved to the baseline agreed during initiation
Product Delivery	A table of the major planned products, confirming delivery (as appropriate) and with notes of any significant deviations from agreed requirements. A detailed log of all *products* and references to quality management records can be attached as an appendix

Project Benefits	A description of the extent to which the **Business Case** is expected to be met, summarising the benefits delivered to date and the prospects for future benefits delivery after closure
Project Performance	An account of the actual performance against the targets and tolerances set for it; including resources, timescales, quality and scope
Lessons Summary	A summary of the principle lessons learned, with a reference to the full **Lessons Report**
Follow-up Actions	A list of the actions needed, with the action owners, once the project has closed

Recommend project closure

When the **Project Manager** believes that the project is ready to be shut down, a recommendation for closure is drafted for submission to the **Project Board**. Consideration is also given to who will be told about the completion of work. This extends to those wider stakeholders who will benefit from hearing a 'good news' story.

Finally, the last loose ends are tidied up, with all of the registers and logs being closed.

Directing a project – the final act

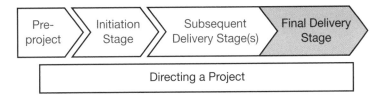

During the **Final Delivery Stage**, the **Project Board** continues to direct a project as it has during previous delivery stages. Ad hoc direction is provided and exceptions are dealt with where necessary. Whilst there's no next stage to approve, there's one additional, final responsibility: to **authorise project closure**. This is the last activity undertaken by the **Project Board** before it disbands.

Authorise project closure

Before giving closure approval, the *Project Board* satisfies itself that all of the project objectives and delivery commitments have been met. The review includes ensuring that:

- the *End Project Report* provides an accurate picture of performance data and what's been delivered;
- the *Benefits Review Plan* and *Business Case* accurately reflect the final benefits position;
- ownership of follow-on actions has been accepted.

The *Project Board* may enlist assistance from *Project Assurance* to confirm the accuracy of the information presented. Importantly, it's verified that formal customer acceptance has been obtained, including from those taking on support and maintenance responsibilities.

Thought is given to the most appropriate audience for the recommendations contained within the *Lessons Report*, and the best way of communicating with them.

brilliant tip

Simply lodging a *Lessons Report* in the organisation's vaults or circulating it via email won't create much of an impact. Go the extra mile, and offer to give a pithy presentation to those that could benefit from what you've learned.

The *Project Board* then signs-off the *End Project Report* and final version of the *Business Case*. In consultation with the corporate or programme management team, the *Benefits Review Plan* is approved and handed over to those is responsible for tracking benefits post-project.

The final act of the *Project Board* is to issue a notification of project closure. It then disbands.

Summary

PRINCE2's *Closing a Project* process provides the structure for bringing a project to its conclusion – whether this is the end point originally envisaged or an earlier stop. For a planned closure to go ahead the *Project*

Product Description must have been delivered against and the agreed acceptance criteria met. Importance is placed on a smooth and meaningful hand-over. This extends to demonstrating that outputs are useable in their intended environment and adequately supported. In the spirit of sharing experience, project performance is reviewed and lessons identified.

PRINCE2 process-in-a-box – closing a project

Purpose summary: to demonstrate that a project can be closed because there's formal acceptance it has met its delivery objectives, or it's in a suitable state for early closure

Triggers:

A stage review confirms that the *Final Delivery Stage* is near to completion – or –

The *Project Board* decides to close the project prematurely

Activities	Key management products
● *Prepare planned closure* ● *Prepare premature closure* ● *Hand over products* ● *Evaluate the project* ● *Recommend project closure*	● Finalised *Project Plan* (with actuals) ● Finalised *Benefits Review Plan* ● Finalised registers and logs ● (Draft) *project closure notification* ● *Lessons Report* ● *End Project Report*

End result: A recommendation to close the project is issued to the *Project Board*

The *Project Board* reviews the basis on which the *Project Manager* is recommending closure, and confirms that owners have been found for benefits review activities and any other actions required post-project. It wraps up its role with a notification of project closure.

Despite tackling the final days in detail, PRINCE2 stays silent on the topic of the traditional end of project celebration. Fortunately, most seem capable of meeting to swap war stories over a few light refreshments without a prompt from the PRINCE2 manual.

CHAPTER 11

The final word

The magic ingredients for success

Some people like my advice so much that they frame it upon the wall instead of using it.

Gordon R. Dickson (1923–2001)

Complicated or comprehensive?

As this book demonstrates, PRINCE2 explains in detail how to manage a project from its first day to its last. A lot of ground is certainly covered between receipt of a *project mandate* and issue of the *project closure notification*. Happily, extensive advice is available.

A lifecycle lays out a logical sequence of steps, and specifies the major checkpoints to be navigated. *Processes* empower the *Project Board* to direct, the *Project Manager* to manage, and the *Team Managers* to deliver. Together, they guide a project along its intended path and deal with events that threaten to push it off course.

Each process generates the *management products* needed to plan the work and to control its execution. Further help is provided in the form of activity descriptions for each *process*. These recommend the individual actions to be taken, and identify the input and output *products*.

At first sight, the approach might appear complicated. However, when the dots are joined up, a straightforward picture emerges. In fact, the fundamentals can be drawn up on a single page.

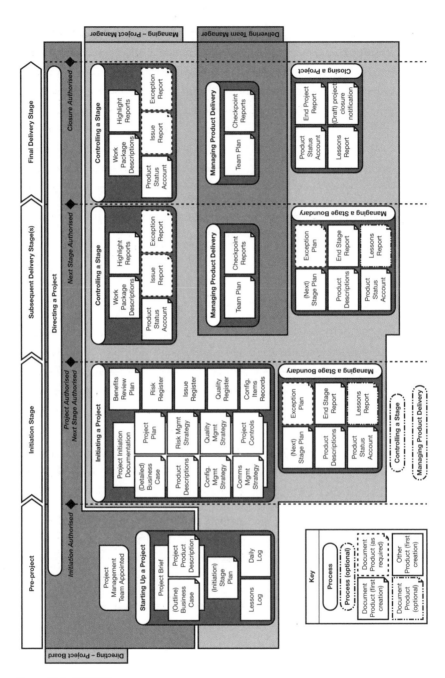

Figure 11.1 PRINCE2 on a page

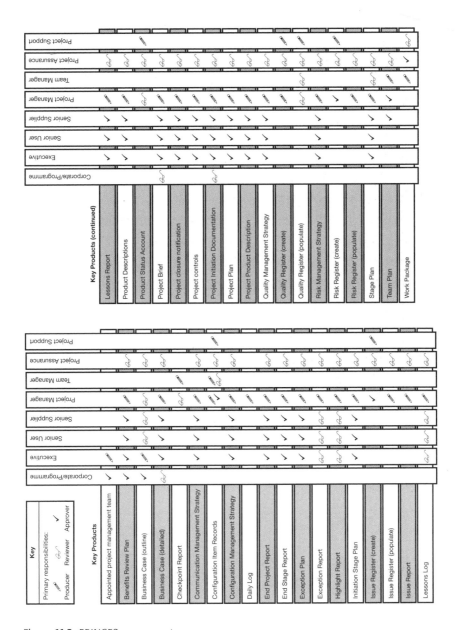

Figure 11.2 PRINCE2 on a page too

Running themes

Instruction on the individual steps to get from A to B is supplemented with management techniques that are invaluable throughout. These are tailored to work seamlessly with delivery processes – and with each other. A *product*-based planning approach prepares for action, and tools are supplied for managing quality, risk and change. Progress reporting mechanisms tie together all of the management controls that operate.

PRINCE2 teams are set up using a common organisational structure, and this establishes an appropriate chain of command. Ready-made roles complement the responsibilities defined within *processes* and for *products*.

Last, and certainly not least, the *Business Case* theme plays a pivotal role from *Pre-project* to the *Final Delivery Stage*. It expands upon PRINCE2's opening *principle* of *continued business justification*, and establishes mechanisms for judging if a project is desirable, viable and achievable.

One size doesn't fit all

However comprehensive PRINCE2's advice might be, it's offered with flexibility. A fundamental *principle* is that the general-purpose method is tailored to suit the circumstances. Intelligent application aligns with existing business practices and standards, and avoids creating a disproportionate management overhead.

Factors such as the size and scale of the venture, and its commercial environment, influence tailoring decisions. Reducing the formality of *products*, combining roles, and adopting more familiar terminology may all be appropriate responses. However, simply omitting parts of the PRINCE2 framework isn't a valid tactic. The method's components are interlinked and so a cut in one area undermines the whole approach.

It shouldn't happen on a project (but did) . . .

Three departments got together to implement an ambitious business change initiative, with the aim of radically improving their collective productivity. Recognising the significant dangers involved, those who commissioned the work mandated that PRINCE2 be adopted. An experienced *Project Manager* was recruited, and she set about preparing plans. Eventually, armed with an impressive set of documents (including a towering stack of *Product Descriptions*), the project launched into delivery.

It soon emerged that only lip service was being paid to the management controls that had been agreed. Rather than delegating authority, *Project Board* members dipped in and out of the detail as they fancied. To make matters worse, in an attempt to placate vocal critics, the *Board* soon trebled in size. The *Project Manager* finally had to accept that however hard she worked, there was only going to be one outcome: project failure. (She was right.)

A partial application of PRINCE2, however diligently applied, misses the point. The strength of the method lies in its integrated approach.

Built to succeed

PRINCE2's thousands of followers gain from using a tried and tested method grown from real-world experience. It's built on sound project management *principles*, and shaped by lessons learned on what contributes to success and the pitfalls to avoid. PRINCE2 comes with a roadmap to follow and a toolbox packed with practical techniques.

Five PRINCE2 features that promote success:

1 Ensuring that the ultimate objective of a project – its *Business Case* – is never lost sight of

2 Keeping the spotlight on what needs to be delivered – *products* are at the heart of just about everything

3 Getting organised with a *Project Board* that provides direction, and a single *Project Manager* that holds the reins day to day

4 *Quality Criteria* in *Product Descriptions* – great for encouraging the quality discussion from the start, and used all the way through to delivery and acceptance

5 The use of stages to break a project into manageable chunks, and with a pause for thought between each one

There are few guarantees in life. However, with a little judicious tailoring and the right team on board, PRINCE2 dramatically improves the odds of a successful outcome.

Index